Thirsk

ffe

or

dborough
ghbridge

River Ure

Husthwaite

Great Ouseburn

Little Ouseburn

Nun Monkton

York

River Ouse

Wetherby

Leeds

ON CALL
with a
YORKSHIRE
VET

JULIAN NORTON

GREAT N ORTHERN

Great Northern Books Limited
PO Box 1380, Bradford, BD5 5FB
www.greatnorthernbooks.co.uk

© Julian Norton 2019

Every effort has been made to acknowledge correctly and contact the copyright
holders of material in this book. Great Northern Books Limited apologises for
any unintentional errors or omissions, which should be notified to the
publisher.

All rights reserved. No part of this book may be reproduced in any form or by
any means without permission in writing from the publisher, except by a
reviewer who may quote brief passages in a review.

ISBN: 978-1-912101-20-7

Design and layout: David Burrill

CIP Data
A catalogue for this book is available from the British Library

For my new friends in Boroughbridge

Contents

Introduction

So here I go again! Another year, another book.

This year has seen me find my feet in a new practice, in the North Yorkshire town of Boroughbridge. It has been a year full of challenges, as I left the practice in Thirsk that I loved, following a corporate takeover. I have had to re-establish myself in a new area, make new acquaintances and develop relationships with new clients – both farmers and small animal owners alike. It has been difficult at times, I have to admit. The out of hours rota is much busier, with many more lambings and calvings and longer journeys to far flung farms a long way from my home in Thirsk. I work a lot harder, with longer hours and this was a change I never expected to have to make.

However, I've found myself a new home, professionally at least. I have been made utterly welcome in this lovely little town and this lovely little practice. The retired senior partner, Alistair Rae called in to see me on my first morning, to shake my hand, to wish me all the best and to thank me. To thank me for coming to join his old practice. "I think you'll like it here," he said.

And he was right. I do like it here and I've enjoyed my first year. I hope I am continuing the "Herriot tradition" that I love so much. As if to cement my place in the local community – a community which makes this town such a lovely place to work – I was asked to judge the "Best Dressed Christmas Window" competition, along with the local mayor. By the time we had been plied with mulled wine in every shop I felt completely assimilated!

This book has been every bit as pleasurable to produce as my previous three – I hope you enjoy it. If you've just picked it up in your local bookshop and flicked through the first few pages to assess whether it's a suitable present for your mother, or to take on holiday to read on the aeroplane, then go on: buy a copy. If you like animal stories from rural North Yorkshire, I promise you won't be disappointed!

Vera's newborn Zwartble lambs.

First Lambing of the Year

4th January

I rolled over, more than half asleep, "Did my phone just ring?"

Mumblings in the affirmative from the far side of the bed confirmed that I'd just slept through a middle of the night call. I'd only been asleep for an hour, but this is the time (the only time) when I am dead to the world. I crawled out of bed, found some clothes and stared at my phone.

It was Mrs Thompson. She had a ewe to lamb. It was down at the sheep sheds. I knew where to go, which was lucky because I was still in a sleepy fog as I wound my way along the dark lanes. The night was clear but the moon was just a thin sliver, so everything was inky. Equally lucky was that I knew the route well. I must have cycled the road a hundred times, as well as negotiating its bends on the way to calls similar to this one over the years. I passed the yard where I had gelded two colts with a previous colleague (or at least tried to – the second one had got up and ran off before we had even started). Then I passed the farm where Graham's heifer had escaped, ran across a field, jumped a stream and made a new home five miles away, with some Limousin cattle. I passed Larry the guinea pig's house, whose lump I had removed only the previous day. Finally, I took a left turn just before the house where Flo the Labrador used to live – sadly I had put her to sleep just before Christmas.

I arrived at the shed without the trauma of getting lost, as I had done a few times over recent weeks, this time using my own, in-built sat nav system, rather than having to rely on the one in my car. That one wasn't great at finding remote farms in the middle of the night.

"It's Vera. She's over here," explained Mrs Thompson, wrapped up in a woolly hat and a scarf, which enveloped pretty much her whole body. In the corner of the barn, a handful of Zwartble sheep were waiting to have their babies. These large, badger-faced ewes had been busy winning prizes all over Yorkshire the previous summer. It was a maternity ward full of champions and their progeny would hopefully follow suit in due course.

"She's been on for a while and nothing's happened," she explained, before adding, "I didn't get you out of bed, did I?"

It was my turn to mumble something as I tugged on my wellies and waterproof trousers.

I lubed my hand and got straight to work. One lamb, seemingly inert, was positioned correctly, but stubbornly refused to move. It needed some gentle and then some firm manipulation, to get it engaged in the pelvis. Moments later, Vera's first lamb was on the straw, thankfully, spluttering to life. The effect of a new lamb on a weary vet was more potent than a double espresso. All traces of fatigue evaporated. I felt for a second lamb. Soon, Vera had twins and both newborns were shaking their heads, flapping their ears and starting to make vigorous lamb noises. I couldn't suppress a huge grin – the biggest one I'd had for a while – it had been a hard few months. I could have lingered on the farm all night, watching the mother fastidiously licking her babies, to clean and dry them and to establish the bond that would last until the autumn. It was a wonderful thing to experience and something of which I never tire. My first lambing of the New Year, in a new practice, had gone like a dream!

Four hours later, awoken rudely by the persistence of my alarm clock, I rubbed my eyes again. Had I been up in the night to lamb a sheep? Or had it all been a dream?

A Goldfinch with Blight?

12th January

"Can someone have a word with this man about his goldfinch?" asked Julie, late one afternoon this week. "He has a goldfinch with blight. At least, I think that's what he said. He's on the phone."

I screwed up my face as colleagues ran as fast as they could in the opposite direction. This was not going to be a typical 5.30pm telephone call.

"Are you sure?" I asked. I thought blight was a condition affecting potatoes, rather than birds.

Julie went back to the phone to get more information about the chap's problem, and was soon back with details.

"It's not blight at all and it's not a goldfinch. It's a *Gouldian* finch and it's going *light*. He said that if you knew anything about birds, you'd know what he was on about!"

I knew about these beautiful finches, although I am not a bird expert. They are lovely, colourful little birds, purple, orange, yellow and blue in all combinations. "Going light" does not mean they are becoming pale, rather that they are losing weight and *becoming* lighter – less heavy. It's a bad thing and is usually connected with serious disease. I went to the phone to see what I could do.

"I'm very worried," the owner of the Gouldian finch told me in despair, "I've phoned lots of vets, but nobody seems to be able to help. One practice I called said I would have to pay £47 up front before they would see the birds. Some have died. Do you think you can help? I have a couple here that'll be dead by the end of the week if they go the way the others went."

I arranged an appointment for late morning the following day. I didn't ask for £47 up front. Even though this bird fancier would be travelling for over an hour to see me, I could tell he was relieved.

"Can you bring the sick ones and also some normal, healthy ones please, just so I can see both?" I asked. "I'm not a bird expert, you see, so it will make it easier to assess their problem."

The following day, exactly at the allotted time, the bird fancier from the middle of the North Yorkshire Moors appeared with a selection of birds – some healthy, some sick and two very sick. I asked various questions and compared the birds visually. It was clear that the poorly ones were not well. They sat on the bottom of their cages, unable or unprepared to balance on a perch. I lifted them up, cupping them in my hands to prevent escape and to allow me to get a closer look. They were so weak that they put up minimal resistance.

Next, to compare, I asked to look at the healthy ones. As if to emphasise the point, the first bird flapped its strong wings, escaped from my gentle grip and flew off. Luckily, I had shut all the windows. There is an urban myth in the veterinary world, about a terrible incident with an escaped bird and an extractor fan. I probably don't need to elaborate and I can confirm that there was no such extractor accident today.

I talked through the options and came up with a tentative diagnosis of coccidiosis, which was actually what the knowledgeable owner had suspected. He was delighted we had come to the same conclusion. I prescribed the appropriate medication – something to go in the water to kill the offending bugs. We crossed our fingers for the sick birds, but also for the rest of the flock, as cases like this can affect the whole aviary.

A beautiful Gouldian finch, mistakenly called a "goldfinch".

Murphy the sleeping puppy.

Tired Vet, Tired Patient, Cat Wound, Horse Wound and a Busy Hazard

18th January

I had been up for much of the night, treating a horse with colic. His name was "Dot Com". I'd been to see him several times over the course of the afternoon and evening. Each time, I measured his parameters fastidiously – heart rate, gut sounds and rectal findings all suggested that the colic was not too serious, but it persisted stubbornly. After each visit, the signs he showed – of kicking at his belly and looking at his flank – improved, only to return a few hours later. His home, on a cold and windy hilltop farm, was beginning to feel like my home as the night wore on. Even between visits, I didn't get much sleep, anxious as I was that the "Dot Com" bubble might burst. Eventually, a phone call at 8.30 the next morning confirmed he was back to normal health.

But, tired as I was after the non-stop night, there was still a day's work ahead. There was a cat in need of attention and another horse to see, standing in a field, lame. I drew straws with a colleague to see who got the outside job in the grim January rain, and who stayed to repair the large laceration on the cat's tummy.

I got the horse visit. It was a long drive to get there, so at least I could relax and listen to the car radio, as I headed south with extra boxes of antibiotic powders – from the conversation on the phone, it sounded like a case of cellulitis.

My afternoon appointment list was a much more relaxed affair – post-op checks, vaccinations, follow up consultations and no major dramas. One of the appointments on the list was every vet's favourite. A puppy called Murphy for his first vaccination. The little Labrador was cute and friendly in equal measure and examining him before administering the protective injections could hardly have been called work. The ups and downs of veterinary practice have a happy way of evening themselves out.

It's amazing how a cute puppy always comes along to cheer you up when you are tired or have been dealing with something sad.

He didn't bat an eyelid as I injected the vaccine, continuing to wag, snuffle and investigate all the interesting things on the examination table. I chatted with his owners, confirming that he was in perfect health and discussing all aspects of puppyhood, offering advice on feeding, a suitable worming regime and socialisation. Meanwhile little Murphy, oblivious to the discussion, which was centred entirely upon him, fell completely asleep on the table. I'm sure it wasn't because he was bored. I wish all the patients were so at home at the vets that they fell asleep! I took a photo, just to prove it. I could very easily have snuggled next to him and closed my own eyes. If I had, I'd have been fast asleep in no time at all!

I woke Murphy up, ruffled him behind the ears and bade him farewell. I'd be seeing him again in a couple of weeks for his second dose of vaccine. I returned to my computer. An extra appointment had been added at the end of the list. It promised to be much less relaxing than Murphy. I read the notes for the dog, who was (amusingly) called "Busy". The owners, in Yorkshire on holiday from Hampshire, were called "Hazard".

"Dog going completely mad," was the reason given for the appointment. A dog called "Busy Hazard", going completely mad. There was zero chance of any sleeping there!

Team Norton

On Thursday mornings, I often get the chance to work with my wife. This is a good thing. We work very well together as an efficient unit. Any minor squabbles about whether the dog's feet are clean enough to enter the house after a muddy walk, or if the Saturday night pizzas have sufficient toppings quickly evaporate when there is a veterinary conundrum to solve, or a serious surgical challenge requiring more than one pair of hands, or more than one set of eyes. There is no faffing and no vacillation when Team Norton is in action. I've worked well with other colleagues in the past. Sue and I, back in Thirsk, were a force to be reckoned with. Ben and I could tackle pretty much anything too, back in those youthful, halcyon days at the start of our careers. But as a veterinary combo, Anne and I are definitely up there.

On Thursday this week, we saw a case that called on our combined powers like never before. That sounds dramatic, but we did a very nifty bit of surgery.

Sid, a middle-aged Labrador was not looking too good. He'd been in a couple of times over the previous few days, having suddenly gone off-colour. He'd improved after each injection, but still, to quote a line from a children's book, "something wasn't right with Sid".

"His back's up," was the accurate, but non-specific sign described by Neil, his owner. I knew Neil from having treated various of his cows, but I hadn't met his dog before. Sid and Neil had been shooting last weekend, reported Neil, but he wasn't aware of anything that might have happened to cause a problem. Sid, however, was certainly sick. He was painful in his abdomen and around his back, and I thought I could feel a mass. X-rays and an ultrasound examination were required.

Both confirmed my suspicions – the left kidney was enormous and clearly full of cancer. Even when he was sedated, it was still painful. I made a call to Sid's nearest and dearest to explain the situation.

"Well I'll leave it to you, Julian," said Neil. "Do what you can, do your best. If it doesn't work out, then he's had a good innings."

So we embarked on one of the most challenging pieces of surgery we had ever carried out.

The last time I'd called for Anne's help was to assist me with a procedure on an alpaca called Ebony. There was a large mass on her lower leg. It was not as immediately life-threatening as Sid's kidney cancer, but it was causing problems and its size and position necessitated its removal. The patient was also elderly, so the general anaesthetic required for the surgery would need careful supervision, possibly including a top up during the procedure. It was definitely a two-vet job. Kneeling together, over an alpaca's leg, in a cold barn was, in many ways, a very different experience to today's operation. It was "work in the field", out on a limb (quite literally), but it was just as rewarding. As soon as I'd placed the final suture and cleaned the area, Ebony jumped to her feet and trotted off across the yard. It was team work in action.

Back with Sid, we carefully dissected the cancerous kidney from its attachments, methodically tying off the abnormal blood vessels supplying the aggressive mass. I looked to Anne again for reassurance. The most dangerous part of the operation was upon us: identifying and ligating the renal artery, as it branched off the aorta. The kidneys receive one-third of all the blood pumped by every heartbeat, making this artery one of the biggest in the body. There was no room for error. I took a deep breath and hoped it would go as smoothly as our last operation together.

Anne and I (AKA Team Norton) working together to remove a lump from Ebony the alpaca's foot.

A Wild Cat Chase

It was very late when the phone rang. A chap, on his way home from the pub (after what must have been a fairly long lock-in) had spotted an injured cat pulling itself into a bush. Judging by the slur in his voice as he explained what he had seen, I suspected he was meandering rather than walking home.

"There's a cat," he said slowly and carefully. "I think it's been hit by a car. It's under a hedge. Can you come…" he paused for a moment, gathering his thoughts or regaining his balance, before continuing "…and help it?"

I'd been in this position before, called to help an injured animal in the darkness of a nocturnal North Yorkshire, only for the patient to slip silently away before I arrived. Injured animals are often bewildered and frightened and their reaction to stress and pain is to run and hide. The most memorable of these incidents occurred many years ago, when my oldest son was a tiny baby. The windows of opportunity for sleep were short; two-hour stretches at most, and in one of these windows, in the early hours of the morning, my pager went off. A traffic policeman had spotted a badger, sitting by the side of the road looking stunned. Despite my assurance that the wild creature was likely to run away before I could get there, the policeman was most insistent I attend. I dragged myself out of bed and set off. Lo and behold, by the time I had made the twenty-minute journey to the stricken badger, it had got up, shaken itself and waddled off into the depths of the night. By the time I got home, baby Jack was awake again!

Anyway, I established the likely whereabouts of tonight's cat and agreed to go and see if it could be captured. Even if an injured animal doesn't run away, catching the patient is not always easy, especially in the darkness of the bottom of a hedge. I called at the practice to collect baskets, blankets, towels and extra painkillers and sedatives, and crossed my fingers.

The first job was to find the animal rescuer. This was easy. He was leaning against a lamp post, which was next to a hedge. His directions had been accurate.

"It's in here," he said, after a brief introduction, pointing to the aforementioned hedge.

We searched the hedge, without any success, so I broadened the net, so to speak, casting my torch around the area and peering under a couple of nearby cars. There it was, sad, forlorn and immobile. The village was silent and all the houses were dark. I didn't fancy knocking on doors to ask people to move their vehicles so I could get to the patient. We set about trying to persuade the cat to come out from underneath the car, using long twigs from the hedge. The cat moved but not sufficiently for either of us to grab it. This continued for many minutes without any progress. The drunk man started throwing small pebbles, but the cat stubbornly stayed put. Eventually, it made a bid for freedom and lurched, dragging its back legs, back to the hedge, where it jammed itself into the base of a privet bush. Using a blanket to improve my chances of grabbing it and to protect my hands from bites or scratches, I managed to scoop up the injured animal and bundle it into the basket I'd brought.

"Thank you for coming," said the drunk man, shaking my hand warmly. "I feel better now. I'm glad we've helped."

"Thank you for calling me," I said. "I'll take him (or her) back to the practice and have a look at the injuries. Then I'll try and trace the owner and work out what to do next."

Hopefully, the injuries would be fixable, the cat would have a microchip and would be back with its owners very soon.

Fourteen Metres of String and a Donkey Penis

13th February

I had spent the first part of the morning treating a donkey. Gary (a strange name for a donkey, I thought) had blood stains down the inside of both his back legs. The blood was emanating from a terrible thing on his penis. It looked like a festering mass – ulcerated, bleeding and sore. Robert, the farmer, was worried. His initial thought was that Gary's penis had been bitten by the over amorous, or over aggressive, jenny who lived in the next pen (a jenny is a female donkey). But the sore had failed to heal with cleaning, ointment and antibiotics and Robert had called for my help.

When I examined it, the sore bit seemed to be more of a lump-like growth, attached to the prepuce, rather than the penis itself. This was both good and bad. Bad because a growth was a worse thing to have than a traumatic injury; good because it would be possible to remove. At least, I hoped it would be possible to remove. I gave Gary a hefty dose of intravenous sedative and made a plan. All eyes were on me, as I thought through the options. The mass was the size of a golf ball and on a stalk. A full general anaesthetic would be required to surgically excise it. On the other hand, some carefully placed "rubber rings", just like the ones used to remove lambs' tails and castrate young calves, might provide a simpler solution. It was worth a go. I set about injecting the stalk of the lump with local anaesthetic. Gary didn't like this, even though I used a tiny little needle. I hoped he would appreciate it in the long run though. I stretched an orange rubber ring over the lump and gingerly nudged it into place, so it encircled the pedicle tightly. I reckoned in a week or so the troublesome lump would be off.

As I got back into the car, my phone pinged with a message from Katy, my colleague, back at the practice. She had sent me a picture of an X-ray, complete with a stone sitting in the subject's stomach.

Surely the cause of the dog's vomiting. Could I lend a hand with the surgery later today?

"Of course," I replied. It would fit in after I'd finished afternoon surgery.

I waved goodbye to Gary and his owners. They promised to keep in touch with the progress of his lump and I headed back to the practice to do my afternoon appointments.

Katy had already started the exploratory laparotomy on the spaniel by the time I popped my head around the door of theatre, halfway through the afternoon.

"It's not quite what I expected," she explained, showing me the plicated and angry-looking intestines. The stone, clearly visible on the X-ray, was not the main problem. A length of string, not obvious on the X-rays, was also stuck in the bowels. This is the worst type of foreign body. A trapped piece of string or thread causes havoc to the intestines, as they contract in on themselves in a futile effort to expel the lengthy object. It was necessary to make numerous incisions in the bowel to remove the string in short lengths. This is the only safe way to remove a linear foreign body, but it is fraught with risk. Making multiple incisions in inflamed bowels is time-consuming and difficult. The risk of wound breakdown followed by peritonitis and death from septic shock is high. Finally, we were there though, and very relieved. As Molly slowly recovered from her surgery, we set about examining what we had removed from the spaniel's stomach and intestines: one stone, about ten leaves and fourteen metres of thick, fibrous string. We'd done our best, now we just had to hope that Molly's intestines would heal.

Julia was just a week old when I met her, whilst treating her father, Gary. Originally, the baby donkey had been named after me, until it was discovered that she was female!

The start of a ski mountaineering race in Glen Coe, Scotland – another busy weekend.

Iodine Deficiency, Ski Racing and Morrissey

26th February

As I left Barry's farm in the darkness of the late evening, both Barry and my colleague Emma looked glum. We'd calved his cow – or rather Emma had calved his cow; I had followed along after evening surgery to lend a hand. By the time I arrived, Emma had managed to deliver the twin calves and did not need my help. Under normal circumstances, a farmer with beef suckler cows would be delighted to have twins delivered and lying in the straw next to their mother, but today neither of the calves had spluttered into life. It looked as if they had both died prior to the onset of labour and it rounded off a bad week for Barry. His calving time had only just begun and already he'd had more newborns flake out than flourish.

I could sense his despair and had made some enquiries to see if I could shed some light on the problem. These twins were born dead, but four other calves had been born healthy over the previous week, only to slide into a terminal decline, despite Barry's fastidious care and attention, and some veterinary help. His herd was of a high health status, vaccinated against all the proper things – Bovine Viral Diarrhoea, Infectious Bovine Rhinotracheitis and Leptospirosis – and no new animals had been introduced. There should have been little chance of disease arriving on the farm. I promised I would give him a ring the following morning to discuss the problems and formulate a plan.

I was worried about iodine deficiency and, after I had talked it all through with Barry on the phone as arranged, I went back to the farm to take the necessary samples. It would be after the weekend when the results came back, so Barry had an anxious wait.

I too had a challenging weekend ahead. Saturday saw my two sons competing at opposite ends of Yorkshire – one at Ponds Forge in Sheffield in the Yorkshire Swimming Championships (where he bagged two golds, two silvers and two bronze medals) and the other at the northern-most edge of Yorkshire, rowing on the river Tees (he won both his races, too). Logistics were, as usual, complex, but at least I didn't have a beeper in my pocket to complicate things.

Later on Saturday night, I went with my sister to see Morrissey in concert at Leeds Arena. The tickets had been a Christmas present. We had both been big fans as teenagers, so it was a great opportunity to hear our childhood hero perform live.

As I drove home afterwards, on the by now very familiar A1, singing the words to his iconic song "Every Day is like Sunday" at full blast, I contemplated how I would manage my Sunday. It was certainly not going to be like every other day of my week.

I was heading to Glen Coe in Scotland and it was precisely four hours until I needed to set off! This time I had a race of my own – the British Ski Mountaineering Championships, organised by the superbly enthusiastic Di Gilbert of Skimoscotland. It was not an easy job to pull myself out of bed, but, standing on the start line, on crisp snow, under blue skies, made the mammoth journey completely worthwhile.

The course was simple – ski to the top of Meall a'Bhuiridh (at 1108 metres) and then ski down again. As quickly as possible. It sounds easy in principle. The fifty-strong field was made up of some of the best racers in the UK, so my pre-journey hopes of a top ten place looked as over-optimistic as usual, especially as most of the guys lined up on the front row had the beards and physiques of mountain goats. I knew they would soon be a long way ahead of me.

There was no gold medal for me this weekend, but it was a lot of fun!

Cute Puppy-Greenstick Fracture. And a Chameleon

7th March

Toby, the little, eight-week old springer spaniel, had suffered a catastrophe. He had been playing outside and an old door, leaning against a wall, had fallen over and landed on his leg. His sad face told the story of a puppy in some pain and he was a pitiful sight as he sat on his owner's lap in the waiting room.

Toby was hard to examine, partly because he was an eight-week-old pup who didn't like sitting still and partly because he didn't like his sore leg being touched. However, this was important to do, because I had to check for a break. A proper long bone fracture is easy enough to identify, because the limb is dangling in an unnatural fashion, defying the normal laws of anatomy.

The first time I ever experienced this was whilst climbing in the Peak District. We were climbing in a small, curved crag, historically used for carving gritstone for use in the local mills. A loud crack echoed around the gritstone amphitheatre. One of the climbers, called Mark, had fallen and landed on a ledge. Another friend and I were the first to get to him, abseiling from the top. He had a compound fracture to the tibia and fibula of his right leg and was in terrible pain. What struck me most, however, was the bizarre angle of his foot, pointing in the opposite direction to the way it should have been. The leg was floppy instead of stiff and rigid, and the departure from that deeply known normality scrambled the brain. For a few moments, half way up that steep crag in Derbyshire, all I could do was stare at the unhealthy sight. Although I have seen many broken bones since then, the sight is still one that my brain still struggles to compute. Bones should be solid and the bottom parts of legs should point forwards.

But Toby's leg was not like this. There was no floppiness and everything was pointing in the right direction. I was still worried

about a fracture though, so I decided to take some X-rays. Small fractures are sometimes stable, for example if the fracture has a spiral shape, or if it is supported by an adjacent bone, in the case of a toe.

Half an hour later we had our answer. Despite the multitude of growth plates visible on the X-ray of a puppy (these are the sites where bone growth occurs and they look just like fractures on an X-ray), it was clear to see the problem: Toby had a hairline crack – a greenstick fracture – half way down his tibia. It would be painful, but fortunately it would heal without any need for surgery. He just needed a big bandage to provide support, and immobility for a few weeks. Toby didn't look happy with his over-sized bandage. But, he looked marginally happier than my next patient, who was not such a common sight in a vet's waiting room in North Yorkshire. My next patient was a chameleon.

His owner was worried about him and, even though I'm no expert in reptiles, I could tell from a distance that he was very lacklustre. He was dull and lethargic as he sat on his owner's hand. I examined him as best I could and we discussed his diet, housing and husbandry. The little fellow was dehydrated and, I thought, had a vitamin D deficiency.

I gave the appropriate advice: chameleons need to imbibe their water in the form of moisture on the surface of leaves in their tank. What was needed, on top of my injection, was a new misting machine, to make proper droplets on the leaves and facilitate better water intake.

Hopefully, in a few weeks, with the benefit of a bandage and a new misting machine, respectively, both patients will be immeasurably improved.

A lacklustre chameleon needing a modification
to his husbandry to solve the problems.

Pregnancy Toxaemia

12th March

Alice was worried about her heavily pregnant sheep. Although she had telephoned to ask for advice, I could tell she really wanted a visit. The flock was due to start lambing imminently and several ewes were looking off-colour. They were vacant, distant, not eating and a bit wobbly. These were vague signs, but ones that a diligent shepherdess, who knew her sheep, would pick up immediately. Most concerning was that one ewe had gone blind and could not stand up.

"I fed them a bale of hay the other day and when I'd unwrapped it, it was quite dusty and smelly," Alice reported anxiously. "Do you think they could have picked up something from bad hay?"

"I think I'd better come and have a look," I replied. "I should be able to set off in about half an hour, although goodness knows how long it will take me to get to you with all this snow."

The picture the farmer painted was serious, and I needed to have a look at the flock. I had only just arrived at the practice when I took the phone call, after a somewhat dicey drive from home. The roads were covered in snow and horizontal blizzards were making the visibility extremely limited. It was anybody's guess how long it would take me to get to the farm, even though it was only about eight miles away.

Thankfully, the gritters of North Yorkshire had done a great job and even some of the smaller roads had received attention. Negotiating my way across the slippery farmyard was the hardest part of the journey.

Alice showed me to the sheep. About ten were penned up in one half of the lambing shed, separated from the others for ease of examination and treatment. They didn't look as bad as I had expected. The worst one, however, was lying in a corner, unable

Snowy weather can cause serious problems for heavily pregnant sheep, particularly a condition called pregnancy toxaemia – a result of a disruption to the food supply.

to stand, her head lolling to one side. It became evident, as I examined her, that the poor ewe couldn't see a thing. This largely confirmed my suspicions. I would need to test a urine sample (difficult in a sheep) or take a blood sample (with the results coming back 24 hours later, at best) for proper confirmation, but a blind, recumbent ewe, heavily in lamb, having just been moved and sitting in a blizzard, was almost certainly suffering from a condition called pregnancy toxaemia. Its colloquial name is "twin lamb disease", because when hill sheep are carrying twins they are particularly at risk. The extra energy demand imposed on a pregnant ewe by the growing lambs depletes her reserves and plunges her into an energy crisis. The condition is often triggered by bad weather (classically snowy weather when sheep are outside and can't find grass to eat), by the stress of being moved or other deviations from a normal routine. In this case, we had snow, recent housing and a change of diet, so the risk factors were all there.

I reached for the largest syringe I had in my car and drew up 60ml of glucose solution. I could inject it straight into her vein to provide an instant burst of energy. Alice and I stepped back to watch her response. It wasn't dramatic. The ewe looked somewhat dazed and confused by the sudden bolus of brain-boosting glucose. She did not stand up, nor did she miraculously start to see. I wasn't necessarily expecting this, but in my mind's eye I always imagine a miraculous recovery. Next, she needed a drench of high-energy drink. We trickled the syrupy yellow liquid slowly into the ewe's mouth. She looked like she was enjoying it and did, thankfully, look more invigorated afterwards. We crossed our fingers, not only for a good response, but also for the rest of the flock to stay healthy. Otherwise it was going to be a very tough lambing time.

The Minibeast from the East

19th March

The message that appeared on my phone at 7.30 on Sunday morning made my heart sink. It was not the nature of the call, but rather its location that filled me with dread. It had been snowing all night and, as I peered outside from behind the curtains, I could see a couple of inches of snow lying on the road and a blizzard in full swing. The ice on the inside of the bedroom window told me everything I needed to know about the temperature. The call was to Dallowgill, right up on top of the moors above Kirkby Malzeard. It was wild up there even at the best of times.

I made a cup of tea and phoned the number on my screen.

"It's our old mare," reported the worried owner. "She's down in the field and she can't get up. She must have been down all night. Goodness knows why she won't use the field shelter like the others. I think it might be time." It was a gloomy assessment.

"I'll be there as soon as I can," I reassured, "depending on the roads. There's been a lot of snow overnight!"

"Oh, they're not so bad. I'm just going to pick up my paper from the shop in the village. If you've got four-wheel drive you'll be fine," came the optimistic reply.

As my journey progressed, the roads got narrower, steeper and more snow-covered but, as predicted, my trusty Mitsubishi had no problems. That is, until the final turn into the yard. It was on a bend and on a slope, and in deep powder snow I executed a graceful ninety-degree spin before slithering to a halt and getting out.

Having introduced myself, I gathered the things I thought I would need – syringes, barbiturate solution, stethoscope and clippers to clip some of the thick winter coat from the old mare's neck so I could see her vein. She was some distance away, lying in the middle of a field in deep snow. It was a bleak sight. With freezing hands, I managed to find the narrowed vein in the old horse's neck and inject two large syringes of barbiturate. There was nothing else to be done, and there was no need for a deep discussion about prognosis. It was quick, painless and peaceful.

I declined the coffee that was on offer afterwards, not because I didn't want one – far from it – but because I was acutely aware that I was on the periphery of the practice area. It would take me a long time to get back and my phone had no signal.

As soon as I was back in range, another call came in. It was another one that would be made all the more challenging by this "Minibeast from the East". The phrase, coined by the media to describe the latest icy blast, made me think of tiny stick insects or crustaceans attacking the country with ushankas on their heads, rather than the bout of snowy weather that was making life so difficult for farmers with sheds full of lambs, desperate to go outside.

And it was a sheep I was off to see next. A cold one, in Nun Monkton. The poor ewe had lambed in the night, then prolapsed her whole uterus, which was hanging out of her back end like a bag of tennis balls.

Down in this village, there was not quite so much snow, but the temperature was just as low and the roads just as icy. I had to unpeel a couple of layers of clothing to allow me to roll my sleeve up sufficiently to reinsert the everted organ. All done, I cleaned my hands in the, now distinctly tepid, water. As I waved goodbye to the farmer, I caught sight of the enormous Maypole in the centre of the village green. Although it was supposed to be nearly springtime, a May Day celebration seemed a world away.

Spring is Coming

31st March

By any measure, the latter part of this winter and the beginning of spring has been terrible. It has been cold, wet and muddy and – unless you happen to like the cold, the wet and the mud – it has been rubbish.

Farmers have been tearing their hair out, unable to get normal jobs done. Their lambing sheds are bursting with sheep and lambs, which would, under normal circumstances, be running around sunny paddocks full of green grass.

I had finished calving a cow, late on Monday night. It had gone well and Robert had another fit and strong bull calf to add to his collection. Almost every time I had met him this winter he had been cheerful and tonight was no exception. After a few early season problems, all was going smoothly and, as I clambered into my car to head home, he told me about a farming friend who had phoned him the previous week.

"He was absolutely fed up, right. Sick to the back teeth with all this wetness, he was," explained Robert.

It turned out that, not only was he sick to the back teeth of the weather, but he was also running low on winter feed. After a long telephone chat with Robert, he was much more cheerful and also better off by five big bales of silage.

"Well, I haven't got masses of silage left either, right," Robert confessed, "but he was just so fed up I said he could have a few of mine. It's last cut silage, but it'll help him out. And after all, spring *must* be around the corner. Otherwise he told me he was going to turn his cows out, but I said, 'NO, don't turn them out when it's like this. They'll ruin your grazing and they'll be chasing grass all summer, right. Have some of mine', I said, and so he's coming to collect it later this week."

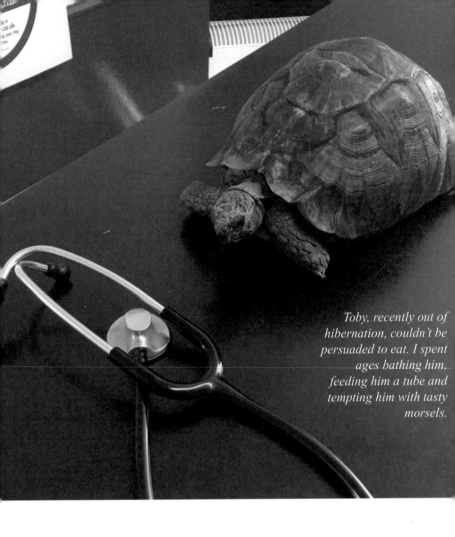

Toby, recently out of hibernation, couldn't be persuaded to eat. I spent ages bathing him, feeding him a tube and tempting him with tasty morsels.

Robert was as wise and as correct as he was generous and uplifting. It is folly to turn out cows when it's as wet as this and yes – spring is (or it should be) somewhere around the corner.

Later in the week, despite continued wetness, flooded rivers and only brief glimpses of sunshine, like Robert, I felt sure spring-proper would be with us soon.

On Thursday afternoon, a large, lidless plastic box was carried into my consulting room. In it was a sixty-one-year-old patient called Toby. Toby was a Hermann tortoise. He had new owners – having outlived his first – and he had just awoken from hibernation. He wasn't eating and his new owner was worried, the burden of responsibility weighing heavily on her septuagenarian shoulders. I measured him and put him on the scales. There is a useful graph for the Hermann tortoise which allows you to work out whether the animal is of the correct weight for its size. Using that graph, I calculated that Toby was definitely underweight. He needed vitamins, warm baths and a special feeding regime to get him ready for summer. He was stubbornly refusing to eat and I sensed there was much work to be done before Toby was eating dandelions like a good un.

I always smile when I see a tortoise. I like them a lot. They take me back to my first day of middle school, when I was just eight. When I came home after that first day at school, my parents eagerly asked what I had been doing.

"We had to draw a picture of our favourite animal," I explained.

"Oh, that's nice. Did you draw a dog?" nodded my mum.

"No. I drew a tortoise," replied eight-year-old me.

There was much laughter. I explained that it was true, a tortoise was not actually my favourite animal, but it was, at least, the easiest to draw. There was a pragmatist in me, even at eight.

Thirty seven years later, whilst I still wouldn't go as far as to say that tortoises are my favourite animal, they are definitely my favourite animal of the non-furry, non-hairy, non-woolly varieties.

My final patient on Thursday confirmed spring was definitely coming.

"It's my young cat. She's rolling on the floor, as if she's in excruciating pain, yowling and writhing. She's in agony!"

"Don't worry," I reassured. "She's just coming into season! We can spay her tomorrow!"

Two Slow Patients

Benji was a shih-tzu – a dog whose origins were on the high plateau of Tibet, where his ancient ancestors would have been guard dogs. The gentle and laid-back nature of these dogs lends itself to guarding a Buddhist monastery and, in another life, Benji would have been the perfect companion to the Dalai Lama.

"He's just not really doing anything," declared his owner, Mr Jenkins, as Benji ambled into my consulting room this week.

"He's stopped eating, and when we are about to go for a walk he looks out of the door, but then he just stands there. If he does come outside then, once he's done his poo, he stands there and won't go any further."

Just as I was about to lift the little dog up onto the table to start my examination, Mrs Jenkins appeared. Moving more slowly than both her husband and Benji, she had not got as far as the door to the room by the time the description of his ailments had begun, although she had heard the start of my consultation and now felt the need to interject.

"That's not true, Roger. He does eat," she protested. "He ate his breakfast this morning and he ate it all. And he does do things. He looks out of the window and he barked at the postman this morning."

I knew where this might end up – I have been in the middle of various marital disputes over the years, about what the dog or cat might or might not be doing. This type of argument rarely ends well and I have learnt that it is better to try to stay impartial. However, Mr and Mrs Jenkins – Enid and Roger – were clearly great companions and, once I had started examining the little fluffy dog, the discussion quickly moved on to different matters, mainly how difficult it had been for Roger to find sufficient daffodils for the arrangements Enid was hoping to make for her local church at the weekend. The disagreement over Benji and his state of inertia or otherwise had passed, and I was relieved.

I was also relieved when I placed my stethoscope onto the side of Benji's chest. There was a loud heart murmur – a whooshing noise every time his heart contracted. This immediately explained the shih-tzu's lethargy. A murmur like this is caused by a leaking heart valve. Instead of closing snugly to prevent backflow when the heart muscle contracts, a leaking valve means some blood goes backwards. Just like a failing plumbing system, this means the heart is not so efficient – there is a build up of pressure at the point of delivery of blood to the heart, and a reduction in its output. This was leaving Benji tired. Happily, I could help him with some heart medication and his signs would be very likely to resolve. Roger and Enid's biggest problem now became the daffodils.

Later that day I had another slow-moving patient. His name was Ayrton, after the famous, and arguably the best ever, formula one racing driver. The name was obviously ironic, because Ayrton was another tortoise. Like Benji, but unlike his namesake, this creature would never be quick. Today he was especially slow, as he had just emerged from hibernation in the fridge.

"I wanted to have him checked over, but I've not been able to find a tortoise expert until now." I felt the weight of expectation as Aytron's owner looked at me. I tried to explain that, although I enjoyed looking after tortoises, I did not class myself as an expert. That said, I did know what was required to make sure Ayrton woke up properly from his winter sleep.

I took the required measurements and weighed him, and compared the results to the graph. He was a good weight and seemed healthy as I examined him as much as it was possible, given that 90% of his body was inside a shell! Springtime, for me, was becoming full of lambs and tortoises, but I didn't mind!

Swedes, Lamb Chops and Wagyu

13th April

The passenger seat of my car looked more and more like a stall at a farmers' market as this week wore on. My collection of produce started with a pair of swedes, given to me by Brian, a farmer I had not seen for some time. We have always bought our Christmas turkey from this lovely farming family and, when our boys were smaller, it was something of a tradition to go up to collect the enormous bird on Christmas Eve. I would be given tea and Christmas cake, while the boys would be plied with jelly babies. I was just leaving the farm, when Brian asked,

"Would you like some swedes?" I misheard him and I thought he was offering me some sweets, just as he used to offer them to my kids at Christmas.

"Thank you, Brian, that would be very nice," I replied and my collection of produce began.

The next addition was two lamb chops. My enthusiastic colleague, Candela, had spent the evening lambing a sheep for another old friend of mine.

"How did the lambing go, Candela?" I asked as we both arrived at work the following morning.

"It was great. I got the lambs out ok, and then the farmer said he had something for you and gave me these lamb chops!" She held out a bag. "And I thought, 'That's charming. It's me who's lambed the sheep and it is you getting lamb chops!' Anyway, then he went and got some for me and said, 'Thank you very much. Here are some lamb chops for you,' which was nice. I ate mine for tea last night."

I put my chops in the fridge for later, alongside the two-pint bottle of fresh, raw milk from Cow Corner in Pickhill, which I'd bought on the way past from another visit. Their milk is delicious, fresh and creamy and perfect for making rice pudding. I've been given the instructions for making mozzarella cheese, too, though this seems way too ambitious if you ask me!

The next day, I added a tray of eggs to the swedes on the passenger seat, but it was a visit on Thursday, to disbud some calves, that provided me with the most interesting food. My first patient looked like any other three-month-old Charolais-cross calf but, Mike explained, this was not just any old calf. It was half Charolais, half Wagyu. Wagyu (pronounced "wagu") is not some kind of tomatoey meaty sauce for a Roman emperor in a Monty Python film. It is actually a breed of Japanese bovine, which provides tender meat with a buttery, soft texture on account of the marbling of fat throughout the meat.

In Japan, these cattle are treated like royalty. They get to wear jackets when it is cold, have names instead of ear tag numbers and eat tasty rice straw. They grow slowly and take three years to fatten, which is about twice as long as typical beef breeds in the UK. There are stories of the animals being massaged daily and offered beer to drink to ensure that they are completely relaxed, but I suspect these last two facts might not be real.

Mike assured me that this particular calf (although he was impeccably behaved and extremely relaxed during the disbudding procedure) had not enjoyed beer or daily massages. I finished off the rest of the jobs before I left, Sarah, Mike's wife, handed me a large, vacuum-packed joint of Wagyu/Aberdeen Angus topside. It looked delicious and I thanked them both profusely for the generous gift.

"I see you are collecting farm produce," commented Sarah when she saw the swedes and eggs in my car.

"I seem to be!" I replied. "The perks of being a vet, I suppose – although I'm not sure I can combine all these ingredients into the same meal!"

Villages of Yorkshire

19th April

Anything and everything can happen on a Saturday morning and this week was no exception. Friday evening had been quiet, but a quiet evening is often followed by a busy day and so it happened.

I had arranged a visit to a dairy herd, in the pretty village of Markington, to check on some cows. I had not been to the farm before, but I knew how to get to the village, as I played cricket there many years ago. As I recall, it was a successful game. Bagby Cricket Club, for whom I played, was a force to be reckoned with back then. Its fast bowlers, agile fielders, tenacious batsmen and finger spinners who could bowl all day made the small club a tough team to beat.

I set off in good time, accompanied by enthusiastic vet-student-to-be Rosie, the daughter of a local farmer. It is good to get students out on visits, although in these health and safety conscious times, it doesn't happen as often as it should, making it tough for the youngsters to gain experience. Rosie and I also needed to discuss her university choices. She had three offers from vet schools and I wanted to talk them over with her.

However, before we got to the farm, and even before Rosie and I got onto the topic of vet schools and their respective merits, there was a phone call from the practice: "Could you go to see Mr Shipton, Julian? He has a sheep to lamb and its head is back." Luckily for me, Mr Shipton's farm was in Burton Leonard, which was, with only a minor diversion, on my way.

The elderly farmer waved my car onto the one dry place on the farm, before showing me to his sheep.

"Have you some water, please?" I asked, which is always one of my first questions when I arrive to lamb a ewe.

"Aye, over they'er." He gestured towards a metal water trough.

My heart sank. It was hardly a warm and clean water supply, but it was passable with a good squirt of antiseptic in the bucket.

Rosie held the ewe for me (Mr Shipton had gone to feed the other sheep and lambs), as I felt inside and manipulated the head into position so I could deliver first one, then two, slimy, meconium-stained lambs. They were fit and well and soon making lamb noises, and we got on our way to see the cows in Markington. But, there was another call from the practice:

"Can you give Mr Jones a call please? He has a horse with colic and it's down in the field." Phone reception problems meant the call had to wait until I had finished the cows, but they were quickly examined and injected, and I found some signal to make contact with the owner of my next patient.

"You're in Collingham?" That was miles away, with Harrogate and its busy Saturday morning traffic stubbornly standing in my way. At least Rosie and I would be able to cover all aspects of choosing the best vet school!

"Yes, that's right. He's down in the field and not moving. I'm up the lane and right at the top of the hill. Do you know it?"

I knew the village but not the yard, but Rosie was frantically nodding her head, to confirm that she could direct me. "My best friend lives up there," she said. Thank goodness I'd taken her along.

"I'll be there as soon as I can," I reassured the worried owner.

The final visit of the morning took me to Aldborough, just outside Boroughbridge, to see a heifer with a grapefruit-sized lump under her jaw. Another interesting case, concluding a lovely morning tour of some of the prettiest villages in Yorkshire.

BAS and PDG

28th April

Lambing and calving are still keeping us busy in and around Boroughbridge, while our small animal patients continue to present us with many and varied challenges. Obi the Labrador has persistent blood in his urine, which seems to be confounding us all, Ruby the ever-cheerful retriever puppy has undergone surgery to remove a sock from her stomach, and Maisie the fox terrier has been struggling with a complicated pregnancy.

Maisie was on my mind as I set off for the Alps last week. She was scheduled as my first patient when I returned.

I have a passion for ski mountaineering and this, my latest adventure, took me to Zermatt, to compete in the Patrouille des Glaciers (the PDG) – a 60-kilometre ski race which climbs over 4000m through the mountains between Zermatt and Verbier. It is organised by the Swiss army every two years, and is reputed to be the hardest endurance team race in the world.

This was our second attempt at the race. It was cancelled in 2016 due to dangerous weather conditions, literally as we were walking to the starting line. This time though, the weather was perfect and there was no turning back as Francesca, Dave and I made our way to the start, helmeted and harnessed up in anticipation of the enormous undertaking that lay ahead.

Standing on the start line, at half past eleven at night, I felt mildly out of place amongst the hardened individuals who spent their lives up in the Alps. But I was in my element. I love the mountains and I love a challenge and the next fourteen hours promised to be full of both these things.

For the first couple of hours we climbed up, out of Zermatt, before roping up and continuing to the highest point – a peak called "Tête Blanche" at 3650m. It was high enough to be both very cold and

The Patrouille des Glaciers – at the end of an epic race. This is reputed to be the hardest team race in the world. At the finishing line in Verbier, with my teammates, Francesca and Dave, we were in no position to disagree!

a tad short of oxygen. The top section was icy and steep, demanding full concentration. Various other competitors would periodically slide downwards, past me and towards the glacier below. It focused the mind. At least there was no wind, a small mercy. The next section was tough. We had to ski down, off-piste, roped together to avoid the danger of crevasses, in the dark. This was very exciting and more successful than we had hoped – we only crashed twice!

Onward and downward, then upward, then down, then up again, many times. After fourteen hours and nineteen minutes of racing we arrived, sunburnt and exhausted, but exhilarated, in the middle of Verbier. We hugged on the finish line, with just a few tears of emotion, and resolved never to do it again!

I was delayed on my homeward journey, so I had to rush to the surgery, straight from the airport, for Maisie's final ultrasound scan to check her pregnancy. All looked good, which was a huge relief, and the following day she delivered two healthy pups.

As if this didn't constitute a sufficiently varied week, my next appointment was with the farmers of North Yorkshire, at the Boroughbridge Agricultural Society Dinner. I swapped my tight-fitting, go-faster Lycra ski suit for a jacket and tie, and lined up outside the Crown Inn, Roecliffe, for my first taste of this exclusive society. The BAS claims to be the oldest agricultural society in the country and has a membership of exactly fifty. New members are only admitted when a vacancy arises. I had been invited as one of just five guests. I quickly realised that most of the fifty members were elderly gentlemen and that a "vacancy arising" was something of a euphemism.

As the main proceedings came to a close, the president came over for a chat. "I wonder if we might have a new member here?" he said to the group at the table where I was sitting, nodding towards me. I wasn't sure how comfortable I was with the thought of waiting for a casual vacancy!

The Rivers of Yorkshire

4th May

Ever since I was a boy, when a long Sunday dog walk with my father would take us to the confluence of the Aire and Calder near Castleford, Yorkshire's rivers have enthralled me. I think it is fascinating to plot the course of water, as it falls as rain up in the Dales and on the Moors, then makes its way to the Humber. It's easy to ignore the meandering of a river these days, travelling as we do by car, but whenever I cross a bridge I try to think of the river and work out its route towards the sea.

This week, such has been the variety of my work that, on my calls, I have encountered many of the rivers in the county.

Early in the week, I had several trips up into Nidderdale, following the road from Ripley to Pateley Bridge, first to see a poorly alpaca (sick after a difficult labour), then a cow with a twisted stomach, just below Brimham Rocks, and finally to attend to a llama with a nasty growth in his mouth. For my weekly river "tick list" that was the Nidd covered.

The Ure is ever-present for me, now that I am based in Boroughbridge. Walking the dog at lunchtime or, better still if time allows, getting in a quick run, I see this river every day. It is an impressive but gentle river. At Nun Monkton where the Ure (called the Ouse at this point) meets with the aforementioned Nidd, I went to see a dairy herd, a sheep with a prolapse and to cleanse a beef suckler cow. The term "cleansing" a cow suggests gentle bathing in pleasant smelling soap, but sadly the reality is quite the opposite, since this job involves removing the fetid, stinking retained placenta which has failed to detach from the cow after it has given birth. It is a smelly job. The lingering odour only slightly marred my visit to this lovely little village, which also boasts the country's tallest maypole (although my friend from Barwick-in-Elmet begs to differ). Ure, tick. Ouse, tick.

On Wednesday, I went to treat another gelding with colic on the hills overlooking Otley. On the hillside above the village, I had excellent views over the Wharfe, its meandering valley and its Red Kites on not just one, but three occasions. Smartie was suffering from a pelvic flexure impaction which necessitated several visits and several doses of laxative, given by stomach tube, to shift the firm and painful mass of faeces stuck fast in his colon. He was a much-loved pony and was very poorly, so we were all relieved when his pulse rate dropped and his bowels relaxed. Wharfe, tick.

Skipton-on-Swale was on my list of visits on Thursday. A bloated bull was the lucky recipient of my stomach tube on this occasion. The fully-grown animal had gorged himself on barley and it had rapidly fermented in his stomach. As the gas, formed as a consequence of this fermentation, hissed out of my pipe, the Simmental looked considerably more comfortable and his previously drum-like abdomen was soon rendered slimline. It was a satisfying job – just as satisfying as the addition of the Swale to my collection of the rivers of Yorkshire.

The county's most northerly river – The Tees at Yarm, is some way out of the practice area, so that one escaped my veterinary visits, but my son Jack can tick this one for me, as he rows on it almost every day, and last Sunday saw him win the "Tees Rowing Club mini head-race".

To complete my collection, I could just do with a trip to see a farmer in West Yorkshire…

Lucky the Piglet

11th May

"We've been up all night with her. She's had six piglets but there is another one in there. I can feel it with the tips of my fingers, but I just can't get it."

This was the start of a rather fraught conversation I had on Wednesday morning, not long after I'd arrived at work and just as I was about to anaesthetise my first surgical patient. It was always going to be a busy day but, with a visit to farrow a sow at a distant farm, it had suddenly become much more so.

"I'll be with you as soon as I can, Chris, once I've finished this op." I tried to reassure the farmer, who was palpably worried about the final piglet. My radio interview, scheduled for 10am, would have to wait for another day.

I finished the operation and headed out, armed with plenty of lubricant and (I hoped) sufficient good fortune. I couldn't remember the last time I had farrowed a sow – they are usually pretty good at giving birth by themselves and it is something of a last resort to call in the vet. Commercial pig units would rarely do such a thing, but Chris's pig (who was called Sadie) was a special pig and so were the piglets. It is a challenging job to deal with a difficult farrowing. Yes, the piglets are bullet shaped, streamlined and slippery and, under normal circumstances, they shoot out like little bars of soap. But if there is a problem, they are very hard to deliver. A sow's uterus is long and it has two horns. Long arms are needed. On top of this, the slippery bullets are hard to get hold of, so manoeuvring them into the lower part of the birth canal can sometimes be almost impossible.

When I arrived on the farm – a haven for rare breeds: Oxford Sandy and Black pigs, Whitebred Shorthorn cows, Highland cattle, Kerry Hill and Hebridean sheep – I was greeted by two very tired

farmers.

"Kate was in her nightie trying to deliver the first one, at 2am," explained Chris. I didn't need any explanation. I knew the fatigued expression on my own face told the same story of a disrupted night's sleep – it had been a hectic week. I gave the sow an injection of oxytocin to help with her contractions and waited a few minutes to see if it would persuade the baby towards the action end, but the time passed and there was no sign of any movement.

I pulled up my sleeve as far as it would go, cleaned my arm and then applied lubricant up to my shoulder. In I went, further and further, whilst Chris rubbed Sadie's tummy to keep her comfortable. Past my elbow and still no piglet. At the point at which I could reach no further, I felt the sharp little teeth of the final unborn baby. It was fiddly, trying to manipulate the slippery little pig at full stretch. After ten minutes though, it was in the pelvic canal and the final bit was quick. The piglet shot out and I grabbed her before she hit the ground. Piglets are amazing. I had forgotten just how energetic they are, even within the first few minutes of being born. "Lucky", as she was quickly christened, was soon scurrying around, looking for a teat. Sadie, like all sows, had no intention of licking her newest baby, as a cow or a ewe would, but simply lay down, exposing her more than ample bosom for all the babies to enjoy. It was the best thing a mother could do!

Lucky the piglet was, indeed, lucky to have been delivered safely after a difficult night. He was quickly onto the teat, suckling milk. Nature is an amazing thing, with just a little bit of help needed at times!

Meerkat Accident

17th May

I could hardly believe my eyes as I scanned the daybook to see what the morning had in store for me. The first message said:

JN – Meerkat, possible broken tail. Please phone asap.

I jumped at the chance. I had seen meerkats at the Yorkshire Wildlife Park and I had seen the ones with Russian accents on TV, but I had never had the opportunity to treat one as a patient. I was on the phone in a flash.

"Yes, it's one of my meerkats," said Joe, the owner, clearly very worried. "The others have attacked her and she's very nearly dead. Can I bring her down to the practice?"

I assured him that, inexperienced as I was with creatures from the savannah, I would do my best to help. I also asked him if he could bring a healthy meerkat down as well. Then, if I was in any doubt about what was "normal" I would be able to cross reference (while avoiding a terrible TV ad related pun about comparing meerkats!!).

I wrote the appointment on the computer list and, slowly but surely, the nursing and reception staff realised there was a very unusual animal on its way – they hadn't treated a meerkat before either!

Joe arrived with two cat boxes. One contained "Mia", our patient, who looked very sick. She was limp and weak, and covered in multiple abrasions and dirt. The other contained the normal meerkat, who was quite the opposite – alert, lively and rascally.

Mia had been attacked, in an unprovoked but not unusual fight, as the mob tried to exert their authority upon weaker members of the group. I didn't need X-rays to tell that the tail was broken. It hung, floppy and mangled. If Mia were to stand any chance of surviving this ordeal, the tail would need to be amputated. I took her straight

The first time I'd operated on a meerkat. This was Mia, asleep and ready for surgery to remove a badly damaged tail.

to theatre. It was a calculated risk, putting a shocked animal under anaesthetic, but I reasoned that the sooner the mangled tail was removed, the better she would feel and the lower would be the risk of infection taking hold.

I'd done the same procedure many times on cats, accidentally run over on the drive at home at low speed, and rushed in by a distraught owner ("I didn't realise she was there! She must have been sitting under the wheel when I took the kids to football practice") or, less frequently, on dogs with chronic, indolent injuries to tail tips, failing to heal due to constant wagging. In that sense, the operation was nothing new. People often ask of a veterinary surgeon, "How can you learn about so many different types of animal?" In reality, we don't have to. We use our basic knowledge of anatomy, physiology, pathology and pharmacology, instilled into our brains through the painstaking years at vet school, and we adapt what we know to each circumstance. So, even though I'd never operated on a meerkat before, I knew exactly where to place my scalpel and where to put the sutures.

Everything went remarkably smoothly and soon Mia was looking much better. She went home later that evening, to be housed separately during her recovery and recuperation. It was only later that evening, as I was discussing the remarkable case with a friend, that I realised there might be a problem.

"Don't meerkats use their tails to balance?" I wondered. "I've seen them on telly, sitting up on their back legs to look around. I'm sure a long tail must be important to balance like that."

Then I started to worry. The surgery had been unavoidable, but only time would tell whether Mia would be able to sit up again in that classic pose and survey the savannahs of Great Ouseburn.

Scared of a (Hedgehog) Cake

23rd May

The first appointment of evening surgery had been given a double time slot. It was a simple job – the clipping of a bulldog's nails. I knew the owners and their dog, and was fully aware of the extra time that the consultation might take, mainly because of the chatting rather than the treatment of my patient. But the day was looking busy, so I decided to put it back to a single slot so we could fit in another appointment.

"Oh, hello, Julian," exclaimed Mrs Taylor, as she reached out for the customary hug ("I always like to give my vet a hug," she had said, the first time we met. I must have looked a bit surprised).

"It's lovely to see you again!"

"How's Elsie getting on today?" I asked. "Is it the usual?"

"Oh yes," reported Mrs Taylor. "She's doing fine. Ears all good and her eyes are back to normal too, thank you."

Digressing slightly from the clinical matter of Elsie, Mrs Taylor's husband, Derek, asked, "That young man Ross, your cameraman. He must be a good golfer, is he? I've just met him in the waiting room. We've arranged to go for a round next week. He tried to have a bet with me about who would win, so I think he must be good. He's Scottish too, so I bet he is. I'll let you know the result next week. I think he must be a *hustler*."

I had to admit that, though I had got to know cameraman Ross very well over the last six months, I'd never heard him talk about playing golf. I wasn't sure he was quite as good as Derek suspected.

After a bit more discussion, we moved on to Elsie. She was a typical bulldog, just like the one in the insurance company advert. I'd come to know her well – she came in for a check-up every

month and Elsie and her owners had struck a chord with me. Her nails grew in strange directions and needed clipping frequently, so it was often a quick and easy job. Once the simple veterinary tasks had been completed, we had plenty of time (even within the constraints of a ten-minute consultation) to discuss all manner of other issues – whether canine, veterinary or otherwise. This month's topic of conversation topic, apart from the forthcoming golf event, was more unusual than most.

"A very funny thing happened to Elsie last week," began Mrs Taylor. "You will laugh, because we did. It was so funny. It was Derek's birthday and our friend, the lady who cleans for us, made him a cake. It was a lovely cake – it tasted lovely, didn't it, Derek? – and it was in the shape of a *hedgehog!* This took us by surprise, because Derek isn't so young and we thought cakes in the shape of animals were mainly aimed at children, but anyway that was what she made."

I nodded, slightly surprised by the idea of a wild-animal-shaped-cake for a man, surely in his sixties.

"But the funny thing was," continued Mrs Taylor, "and this is what will make you laugh, Julian. Elsie started GROWLING and making such a fuss. She thought it was a REAL hedgehog and tried to ATTACK it! We couldn't believe our eyes. The poor dog was very traumatised and quite upset. I had to lift the cake onto the side and cover it up with a cloth. Derek had to take Elsie for a walk to calm her down."

I looked down at stocky, if not to say rotund, Elsie, standing stoically by the door of the consulting room waiting to go home. It was hard to imagine that anything, let alone a cake in the shape of a hedgehog, would cause her any alarm at all.

Elsie the bulldog was a good friend. She was a stoic character, but clearly had a dislike of animal-themed cakes!

A worried owner listens to her horse's intestines. I like to give people the chance to use a stethoscope abnormal noises are interesting to hear.

A Day of Horses

28th May

Saturday was a day of horses. Mixed practice is inexplicable. You would think that the law of averages would result in a fairly even distribution of different types of patient, with a few seasonal variations but, during this weekend on call, the horses just kept on coming.

I saw five on Friday evening and that really should have been my quota. But Saturday was also full. It took me back to my Cheltenham days. I lived in the beautiful village of Winchcombe with my girlfriend (who is now my wife). Cleave Hill, the high ground that overlooks Cheltenham, was our backyard and horses were everywhere. Point-to-pointers and racehorses, pony club regulars and trekking yard stalwarts were all treated equally. There were always horse calls, even for those less keen on equine work. Almost all the farms had a couple of hunters and I learned a lot, from both the experienced horse vets in the practice and from knowledgeable yard staff.

So, here I was in North Yorkshire, with a pile of horse calls to do. Firstly, a Hanoverian hopping lame near Almscliffe Crag. His off-hind was throbbing and, luckily for both of us, after a bit of probing, a dribble – if not to say squirt – of stinking, grey pus came oozing from the outside heel bulb and the handsome gelding was quickly feeling much better.

Next, another large and lame horse and another back foot – the worst foot to be painful. Trevor was just as lame but suffering from severe cellulitis. It was sore and he didn't like it being examined. It didn't require my hoof knife, which was a good thing because I did not fancy my chances of holding his leg up to pare away at his sole. A couple of injections set him on the path to recovery. I arranged to check him again a couple of days later – cellulitis like this can be stubborn to fix.

The third case was an odd one, giving me cause to scratch my head. It was also causing all the horses on the yard to scratch. I'd been there earlier in the week and taken photos to show to an online equine veterinary forum for advice. I started some speculative treatment but, after three days, the signs had not improved and there was no consensus amongst my colleagues as to the most likely cause. The eight horses, none of whom had direct contact with one another, had various itchy skin lesions, consisting of scabs, baldness, smelliness, greasiness and oozing. It certainly had the hallmarks of something contagious, but I just could not pinpoint the cause. I was back on Saturday to collect samples to send to the lab. I planned to check some of these samples myself too, in the practice laboratory. This would not be as accurate or detailed as a professional pathologist would be, but at least it would be quicker. But before I could swap my overalls for a lab coat, I had another call. An elderly mare was depressed and not eating. Her owner was worried.

Even from the end of the paddock where I'd parked my car, I could tell the horse was sick. From what I could see, I had an idea of what the problem might be. My examination added to my suspicion that the mare was suffering from grass sickness. She had a high heart rate, profound depression and very little gut motility. These were all indicators of this serious and mysterious illness that causes paralysis of the intestines of a horse.

"Can she eat or drink?" I asked.

"No," was the reply. "She's not had a thing. Well, she tries – she puts her head in the trough, but the water just spills out of her mouth." This confirmed my fear.

I gave her an intravenous injection to provide her with some relief, but I was not optimistic. I went back to recheck her later. We have our fingers crossed.

Electrocuted Herefords and Llama Trekking

2nd June

My first call on Monday morning was not very pleasant. The two in-calf Hereford heifers were lying, bloated, under an electricity pylon. Even from a distance it was clear that they were way past the point at which veterinary intervention would have been useful. There was no hope of reviving the two electrocuted animals. I simply had to confirm their identity and give a diagnosis. I had pregnancy tested these two lovely heifers just a couple of months before, along with the rest of the small herd and, at that point, everything to do with the cattle was rosy. All were pregnant and the farmer and his wife, after enjoying a smooth calving time, were both looking forward to a summer with young calves. Their numbers would be depleted because of this tragic accident.

The pylon was a small wooden-pole type, with a conspicuous metal cable anchoring it to the ground. Somehow, electricity had jumped from the wires and surged to earth, via the two heifers. It is not so uncommon to see cattle killed by lightening or electricity. I have spent many hours visiting farms after electrical storms to confirm death and establish the circumstances surrounding it. Bovines seem to have an uncanny ability to conduct electricity to earth more easily than anything else nearby. I remember one time – the worst – when a whole row of heifers were dead, having been standing in a large puddle next to a metal gate when the lightening struck. It was a terrible sight. Today, as always in these situations, I needed to satisfy myself and the insurance company of the true course of events.

There are stories from James Herriot's books which tell of farmers using candles to recreate burn marks on animals which had died from other causes, in an attempt to dupe the insurers. I think a combination of veterinary experience and the discovery of candlewax usually led to the correct outcome in the end!

A selfie with a llama before we go on a family llama trek. I think the llama looks calmer.

There was no candlewax here and no such insinuation. The nearby village had suffered a power cut the previous night, presumably as the electricity went to earth through the cows and not to iPod chargers or mobile phones. I could imagine the annoyance on a Sunday night as houses went dark, tellies fell silent and phones were switched to "low battery mode", the locals unaware that the cows had also fallen silent. A temporary loss of power was nothing compared to the grim reality on this farm on Monday morning.

Happily, things got better later in the week. I had some much-needed time off and my family and I took the chance to go llama trekking. Nidderdale is not a place that you would normally expect to see llamas, but that was exactly where we were. Even on a sunny day it felt a long way from the high Andes, from where these animals originate.

I have been looking after the llamas at Nidderdale Llamas for a while and, after various ailments and accidents, this trek was by way of a thank you from Suzanne, their owner. My sons, Jack and Archie, and I had taken alpacas for a walk once before. That had been an unusual afternoon, but very entertaining, and I, for one, was looking forward to my second camelid encounter. The boys were not completely convinced, but after some persuasion (not to say bribery), off we set.

The first task was to allocate llamas to people. This sounds strange, but llamas have very distinct personalities and matching the wrong animal to the wrong person can spoil the day. Jack was given one called Toby – a "confused" llama, never sure exactly what he should be doing. He needed a quiet confidence and leadership that Suzanne perceived my oldest son could give. Archie took Chester, a very well-behaved, but cheeky and mischievous llama who loved a conversation. An apt pairing if ever there was one.

I'm not going to tell you the personality traits of the llama that I was given…

Four Feet and a Vet Student

10th June

It was another night on call and another date with Netflix aborted. A cow was calving, but from the message it sounded more like a sheep lambing:

"I can feel four feet and a head. And she's trying to prolapse, too!"

Ryan was an experienced farmer with a fantastic herd, but he was flummoxed this evening. So were all his family and Erin, a vet student who was spending some time on the farm gaining some hands-on experience. When I got out of the car, late last Wednesday evening, there was quite a crowd waiting for me. The calving was destined to be a challenging one and held the promise of an entertaining hour for the onlookers.

The cow was lying comfortably, but on a slope. The weight within her abdomen and the angle of slope were compounding one of her problems – a pineapple-sized rectal prolapse. Bizarrely, the water bag, usually the shape and size of a melon, looked more like a party balloon, extending as it did a good three feet from the cow's vulva. I wish I had managed to take a photo, but there wasn't time. As I made my examination, it became clear that the water bag was extruded into this elongated shape because of other strange arrangements inside the cow. The vaginal wall was being pushed outwards, also in a bizarre fashion and, lo and behold, as I felt inside the cow, I encountered one, two, three and then four feet. Also, a head! This was all very unusual and even though the cow was obviously in a pickle, the whole thing started to assume a vaguely comic aspect.

I called for Erin to have a feel. I hadn't asked at what stage of her veterinary education she was. She might have been a first-year student – naïve and green, or in her final year, on the verge of being in the same position as me.

"Have you ever felt inside a cow before?" I asked. There was vigorous head shaking, but a huge grin appeared on her face, which persisted for the rest of the evening. This was invaluable experience for a vet-to-be and I wasn't going to let the teaching opportunity pass.

The next job was an epidural to stop the straining, numb the area and make manipulations more straightforward. I needed all the help I could get to untangle the jumble of legs and heads I could feel.

"Erin, have you ever done an epidural injection before?" I asked, returning her grin. I knew the answer. Again, vigorous head shaking. I talked her through the process, clipped and cleaned the area above the cow's tail and showed Erin exactly how and where to place her needle and syringe. It worked a treat, as proven by the sudden flaccidity of the cow's tail.

Now to sort out the internal problems. I decided to repair the rectal catastrophe first and I explained this to the onlookers. "Everything will be easier with this pineapple back inside the rectum," I declared, to a gale of laughter from the spectators.

That bit was easy to fix. Next, I needed to unravel the legs. It took me some time to work out what belonged with what, but I aligned one set of legs with the head I could feel, applied the ropes and pulled. The little calf shot out with ease and was soon lying where the party balloon water bag had been.

I felt for another baby – the first was small and I suspected twins. As predicted, the twin was there, lined up and ready to be born.

"Erin, have you ever delivered a calf?" I asked. Erin was cleaning her arm and applying lubricant before she had answered.

It had been a good night for the young veterinary student!

A Lesson in Health and Safety

14th June

Over tea on Monday evening, my wife was bemoaning the daily health and safety conundrums that face us, as veterinary surgeons.

"I'd just signed the form to say that I understood that no-one should lift anything over 15kg," she recounted, "when a client with a labradoodle proudly announced that the dog was still healthy and maintaining his weight of 34kg – and hoisted him onto the examination table, before I could stop him!"

"Oh well," the owner had laughed. "It wasn't me who signed the form, so I'll get away with it!"

Thankfully, the examination went well and nobody had a sore back.

It had been a day of health and safety issues for me too, as I went about my farm visits. Sunstroke was one hazard. Severe dehydration was another – beneath my waterproofs, my trousers were wet through with sweat within fifteen minutes of starting my first job. Handling cattle through a crush sounds very safe and usually it is, but the two old farmers handling the cattle were not as quick as they had once been, and I was anxious about the prospects of everyone making it to the end of the morning unscathed.

"I think I need to go for a lie down," I kept hearing from the far end of the yard. Luckily, the cattle in question were impeccably calm and so slow that the risk of melting in the thirty-degree heat was a bigger danger than any marauding escapees.

I have had all sorts of injuries over the years: scalpel cuts to fingers and hands as an animal moves unexpectedly, kicks to places that I cannot describe, arms trapped and bruised between animals and unyielding gates. Once I injected one of my fingers with tuberculin, just above the knuckle. It swelled up so much that, had

Dairy heifers enjoying summer grass,
oblivious to any health and safety issues.

I been a cow, I would have been condemned to slaughter as a positive reactor. Luckily, I survived, but, as I recall, the painful swelling lasted all summer.

Back to Monday, and, apart from losing about a litre of sweat into my trousers, I had escaped serious injury on my first farm visit of the day. The second was uneventful, even though the farmer was sitting on the beach somewhere in the Balearics when he called me, anxious about his heifer.

"She'll be in the yard when you get there," he explained. "It'll be easy to get her in the crush and have a look. My friend is looking after things whilst I'm on holiday and he says we need a vet out. I'd be grateful if you could go as soon as you can. She's my favourite heifer, you see."

Despite the friend not being adept at handling cattle, it was fine. The heifer trotted into the handling system like an old pro. There would be no danger here.

My final visit was to examine a couple of batches of much more unruly heifers. The banging and commotion from the first group suggested they were wild and kicking, through resentment at being corralled when they would rather be in the field, enjoying the sunshine. However, as we worked our way through the group, it became evident that the biggest health and safety issue of the day was nothing to do with the heifers, or the heat.

From a hole in the red brick wall adjacent to the cattle crush, emanated a low-pitched buzzing. Tens, if not to say hundreds, of wasps had started to swirl around, angered by the noisy cattle with their quick kicks and, no doubt, annoyed by the presence of a vet and farmer disturbing their halcyon summer day. I could only imagine the consequences of a stray back foot shooting out sideways and hitting that buzzing nest. In the confines of the windowless, musty barn, it would have been many times worse than lifting a dog who weighed over 15 kg!

Prolapsed Vagina and Lacerated Penis

21st June

The life of a vet is a funny one. Some weekends – like the one I had a few weeks ago – are filled with horse calls, for no particular reason. Others, sadly, are filled with euthanasia cases. Recently we put to sleep a rabbit, a goat, a dog, two sheep and three cats in the space of a couple of hours. One weekend I did three bitch caesarians on a Saturday afternoon, one after another. There was an infamous night when I replaced three uterine prolapses on three different cows at three different farms, at two, four and six am. You'd almost think there was some sort of higher power orchestrating it all. Sometimes these things follow weather patterns – horses with respiratory allergies always make a May bank holiday weekend a busy one, while foggy, damp and cold days in November precipitate a spate of cattle pneumonia cases, for example. Some people though, suspect a full moon is to blame…

But there was nothing to suggest a cause for the pattern for this week's unusual cases, for this week has been filled with rude stuff. It started on Friday afternoon, much to the annoyance of the camera crew, who'd finished for the weekend. Buster was a cocker spaniel, enthusiastic and eager, but his short legs had not propelled him high enough to clear the barbed wire fence. His low-hanging penis had caught on the sharp wire. It was not a pretty sight – blood from a penis makes a lot of mess. Luckily for Buster, the most sensitive part of his manhood had been spared. It was a small gash in his prepuce that was producing all the blood. A carefully placed application of tissue glue soon solved the problem.

Saturday morning brought more excitement from the nether regions. This time Molly – a Rottweiler bitch with a vaginal prolapse. A plum-sized, pink swelling protruded, disconcertingly from her vulva. My colleague (and all the other staff, for that matter, as well as the owner,) were in a bit of a tizz. It looked a

mess. However, I had seen this sort of thing many times before. During a season, under the influence of the hormones associated with oestrus, the vaginal wall sometimes develops hyperplasia, resulting in a swelling that can pop out. Careful lubrication, usually under sedation, can allow the replacement of the everted tissue. Sometimes a suture across the vulva is necessary to keep everything in. In bad cases, I usually administer an injection to stop the season and everything returns to normal within a couple of days.

Molly was as bad a case as I'd seen for some time, but after half an hour of manipulation and some sutures, everything looked better and was back where it should have been.

The final rude problem of the week came in the form of a phone call. A panicked phone call from a friend. A friend who had an adolescent Labrador. An excitable and hormone-driven Labrador.

"Julian, I'm really sorry to disturb you so late," apologised Olivia. "It's Barney. His penis is all swollen and it looks as if his testicles have moved to half way down his penis. I don't think it's right and I'm really worried. His penis is actually stuck out."

I explained that, whilst this looked very strange, it was actually a perfectly normal thing to happen. The swollen parts weren't his testicles, but just a different (and completely normal) swollen part of his genitalia. A cold flannel would help. I suggested that she should consider getting Barney castrated before too long. As I made my way home, late as usual, I reflected on the last few days. As darkness started to descend, I glanced out of the car window. Was that a full moon?

Barney the very handsome Labrador, looking very pleased with himself after his penis problem.

Dog Show

29th June

On Sunday morning, a couple of weeks ago, the alarm went off at 4am. I woke up with a jolt of excitement, as I always do on competition day, and set off for the start line of *"probably the country's toughest cyclo-sportive"* at Camp Hill, near Kirklington. The event was set to cover 200 miles horizontally and 5000 metres (yes, metres not feet) vertically.

I had entered the event, dubbed "The Yorkshire Beast" for three reasons:

i) It sounded like a challenge

ii) The route covered all the best bits of North Yorkshire.

iii) I was sure some of my cyclist friends would be keen to join me. We could tear up the distance in a super-efficient team-time-trial style and the miles would fly by.

Unfortunately, every single one of said cycling friends simply burst out laughing at my proposition. "You must be joking," was the usual next line, once they'd dried their eyes and got their breath back. So, I lined up with hundreds of other optimists on the start line, in a team of one.

From Camp Hill, the route took me through my hometown of Thirsk, then up the first brute: Boltby Bank. I've been up it many times and, steep as it is, my legs were fresh and it didn't pose a serious problem. The hill at the end of Glaisdale was tough, so too Rosedale Chimney, which is always hard – short but a one in three gradient tells all you need to know. Amusingly, there is a sign at the top of this wall, advising cyclists to dismount *when descending* the chimney! Luckily there was plenty of gentle, rolling flat to follow, as I passed Castle Howard, Easingwold, Boroughbridge

Dunsforth dog show on a very sunny day was a fantastic English summer's event. As the judge, I was following in the footsteps of some great vets from the practice – Vic Bean and Alistair Rae. I had some big shoes to fill!

and Markington and headed out towards Pateley Bridge.

I've never found Greenhow Hill too tough, but various bits of me were beginning to ache by the time I got there. Three svelte cyclists in team kit from Nottingham went past me with ease. I saw them again at the village hall just before Kilnsey Crag, as we all stuffed jelly babies in our mouths, washed down with strong coffee, gathering ourselves before the bugger that is Park Rash. I found myself puffing and sweating from Wharfedale into Coverdale. It seemed like an eternity before I slipped into Wensleydale proper and then Swaledale, with another massive hill whose name I can't remember. The final pull from Reeth over to Bedale took in the famous, but actually not too hard, Côte de

Grinton Moor, made famous by Le Grand Départ several years ago. By chance, at this stage I met up with someone I knew, who was out for a Sunday ride.

"You used to treat my cocker spaniel," he explained. I was not expecting to talk about dogs all the way up the final climb, but that is exactly what I did. It distracted me from the pain.

Then, last Sunday saw me lining up for an entirely different competition. This one involved no bicycles, no puffing, sweating nor any need for hydration or sustenance. I was the judge for the Dunsforth dog show – part of the summer fete held every year in this idyllic village. Julie, the organiser, had been trying to persuade me to come along for years, but somehow I have never made it, due to a combination of on-call duties and prior commitments. However, since the role of judging the dog show has always been undertaken by a vet from the practice in which I now work, this year I felt I could offer no excuses. The late Vic Bean, amazing man and veterinary surgeon, shouldered the responsibility for many years, followed more recently by Alistair Rae, who was Vic's partner at the practice in Boroughbridge, despite his self-confessed lack of knowledge about dogs ("and what breed is this one?") The baton, it seems, has now been passed to me.

I have only judged one dog show before. On that occasion, what I had expected to be a fun-packed event, raising funds for a dog rehoming charity, turned into a very stressful afternoon. It proved impossible to keep everyone happy. This show was different though. Everyone received a rosette of some colour. I was faced with some minor dilemmas, but the "Best-in-Show" was an easy decision. Chips, the most beautiful lurcher I had seen for many years, was a clear winner!

The winners! Tilly and Chips the lurcher (photo with permission of L Spier).

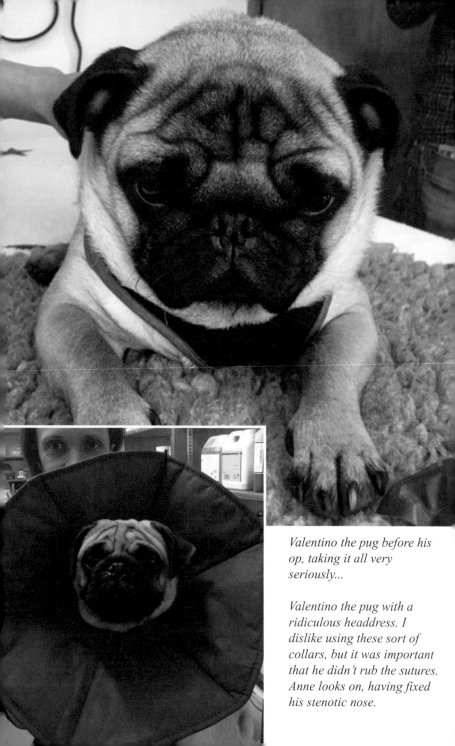

Valentino the pug before his op, taking it all very seriously...

Valentino the pug with a ridiculous headdress. I dislike using these sort of collars, but it was important that he didn't rub the sutures. Anne looks on, having fixed his stenotic nose.

Two Pugs

It has been a week of pugs. The cute, flat-faced breed are endearing, popular at the moment and prone to problems all in equal measure, but I didn't expect to be seeing two in quick succession.

Valentino was a typical pug. He was happy and energetic – at least as energetic as he could be under the circumstances. He liked his walks, but couldn't keep up with the other members of the family – either human or canine. There are some basic design faults in flat-faced breeds, which make it difficult for them to breathe as freely as other types of dog. The nostrils are too narrow and so is the windpipe. The soft palate is often too long and very floppy, which can lead to enlargement of the tonsils and obstruction of the airway. And it all gets much worse in hot weather. Valentino needed some surgical assistance.

I'd checked him over and agreed with his owner that we could help. It was a two-vet effort. Anne, my wife, fixed his narrowed nostrils, having done the procedure several times before. Some deft scalpel action resulted in the same effect on his nose as the strips applied by Olympic cyclists looking for marginal gains. It was my job to make the judgement over how much of the extra, floppy tissue to resect from his soft palate. To take too much away would lead to problems with swallowing, so I erred on the side of caution. Valentino made a quick recovery from his anaesthetic and instantly sounded better. The husband/wife surgical team had worked well. The first time we operated together was on a cow, in the middle of the night, just outside Cheltenham in 1998!

The second pug was called Fiona. She was just as cute as Valentino, and better at breathing but not so good at judging a sensible height from which to jump. She thought she could fly but, having leapt off the sofa, quickly realised that she couldn't. The slightly round dog landed, splat, in the middle of the sitting room and let out a huge yelp.

One front leg was horribly floppy when I examined her. Clearly the leg was broken and it needed plates and screws to affect a proper repair. I am by no stretch of the imagination a "super-vet", but I do relish the challenge of fixing broken bones. It is very satisfying to see a dangling and painful leg stabilised and relatively pain-free, after a couple of hours of painstaking surgery.

Fiona looked much better after the operation. The post-op X-ray showed a sturdy repair and everyone was pleased with the outcome. With the help of Julie, my trusty nurse for the morning, I applied a chunky bandage and left the pug to recover slowly from her surgical ordeal. Dosed up on hefty painkillers and with the huge bandage hindering much movement, she looked a relieved and comfortable but very confused little dog.

I called her owners to report on the surgery and discuss post-operative care. I could not have spoken to happier owners. They'd been on tenterhooks all day. When they arrived to collect their little pug, there were a lot of tears.

"We're so relieved, thank you so much! I just can't wait to have her home. I'll put her in her hoody and she'll spend the evening on the sofa." Fiona was very much loved!

I explained what was required over the next few weeks: bandage changes, controlled exercise and so on.

I just hoped Fiona would not be trying to fly again any time soon, hoody or not.

Howard the Clydesdale

11th July

I knew Howard was going to be a challenge. His clinical notes suggested that his foot problems had been going on for a while, which didn't bode well, particularly as he was probably the largest patient I had ever had to treat. Howard was a Clydesdale – an enormous horse by any standards – so the prospect of keeping his sore foot lifted up for any length of time was a daunting one.

These amazing giants are a type of draught horse, originating from the late nineteenth century when their role was as hard-working agricultural workhorses. Their popularity rose and they were exported all over the world, principally to Australia and New Zealand. Nowadays, of course, their role has disappeared and sadly the breed is in decline. The Clydesdale is considered by the Rare Breeds Survival Trust to be vulnerable to extinction. The weight of responsibility on my shoulders, to sort out Howard's foot, felt significant and literal.

The field was bone-dry and rock-hard under the tyres of my car. This meant it was highly likely that the leathery soles of Howard's feet would be too, which would make my job much more difficult. The other hindrance came in the form of a pig. Gilbert was Howard's friend and companion. The massive horse and the micro-pig were seldom separated. Gilbert wasn't really all that "micro". He had started off as a micro-pig but, just like his equine friend, he had ended up big. He snuffled around behind the limping draught horse.

Luckily for me, Howard, who was a full eighteen hands tall, was as gentle as he was large. I estimated that he weighed about a tonne. He really didn't like his foot being picked up but he wasn't a naughty horse. With difficulty, I lifted the dinner-plate-sized hoof and began making some inroads to the diseased parts of the sole, trimming the black lines of separated tissue, removing anything

bad. I felt like a veterinary chiropodist. In a field, being harassed by a pig. Amusing as it was, it was also hard work – sweaty and demanding on my back. Gilbert was not making life easy, as he rooted around nibbling my shoelaces and stealing my hoof knives. Eventually my paring hit the spot, and a squirt of dark and stinking pus hissed out of a cavity between the layers of hoof. Even in the fresh air of the field the stench was impossible to miss!

I advised my usual hot-tub and poultice treatment, to help persuade more pus out of the hole, but I could tell from the expression on Howard's owner Collettte's face that she didn't fancy her chances. I had visions of the pig chewing the poultice off, in the same way as he had been trying to remove my shoes.

I patted Howard to show my appreciation for him being so gentle and scratched Gilbert behind the ears.

"I've got just the thing for you, Julian," said Collette.

She produced a cold box, out of which she pulled a pair of ice creams.

"This one's for you. You must be hot and tired. And this one's for Gilbert. He loves an ice cream!"

And my rather surreal afternoon in the hot sunshine, paring the foot of the biggest horse I had ever seen, in a field of buttercups while avoiding the attentions of a rather larger-than-micro pig who was eating my shoelaces, ended by sharing an ice cream with said pig. Oh! The Life of a Yorkshire Vet!

This is Howard the Clydesdale, the biggest horse I have ever treated! He was a difficult patient, mainly because of his enormous size.

Not the chicken I was expecting to be dealing with on a Sunday lunchtime! This bird had survived a skirmish with a dog and needed cleaning up.

Chicken at Sunday Lunchtime

17th July

We were just about to sit down for Sunday lunch when my phone rang. I was on duty for the weekend, ever alert to the various animals and their emergencies around the county. This is something that any vet who works on call gets used to. So, too, does their family. I'm not sure mine even notice the beeper going off anymore! They certainly don't raise an eyebrow to find out where I'm heading or what I'm doing!

There was something of an irony in the nature of the emergency that took me away from my Sunday roast – it was a chicken!

"She's been out all night," explained her owner over the phone.

"A neighbour's dog got into the garden last night and attacked her. We thought she must be dead, because we couldn't find her when we got the others in. Then, lo and behold, she appeared just now. She's got a big wound on her back where the dog got her. It looks horrible and I wondered if I could bring her down?"

It sounded nasty and I could tell that the bird was poorly and the owner worried.

We see quite a few "back yard chickens" – the term used to describe a few hens kept in the back garden or in a paddock or stable yard. Apart from the obvious role of supplying eggs, chickens kept like this, away from huge production pressures or the influence of a large flock make surprisingly endearing pets, and form strong bonds with their human owners. In this case, the bird was a rescue chicken, liberated from a previous life laying eggs in a battery cage. It often seems that chickens rescued like this are grateful for a second chance at life and express their gratitude with extra affection.

Hannah and her chicken were waiting for me on the doorstep of the practice when I arrived. I recognised Hannah – she was a veterinary student, back home from vet school for the holidays, and had done some work experience with me a few years previously. This was good, because it meant that I could give an impromptu Sunday-lunchtime seminar and quizzing to the budding veterinary surgeon, about the correct course of action, the most appropriate medication to give and the best route of administration. So, we examined the chicken together.

The wound was deep and nasty. I removed some feathers to get a better look, then gently cleaned off the dead tissue and congealed blood. Things quickly started to look better and the chicken did not seem to mind the intervention.

The next step was to decide whether or not to suture the wound. The skin edges were quite damaged and there was some skin missing, exposing the underlying tissue. It is often difficult to stitch wounds like these in birds, as the skin is so delicate, so we decided that, as long as Hannah could keep the wound clean and protected, nature would provide a better solution, healing the wound by second intention. Painkillers and antibiotics – essential after any bite wound with devitalised tissue – were the order of the day and I drew up the required doses.

"There you go, Hannah," I said, handing the two syringes to her. "Do you know how to inject a chicken?"

Both drugs were expertly injected under the skin and, after a bit of clucking and some poo and feathers on the consulting room table, the patient was deftly tucked back into her cat basket for the journey home. I arranged a revisit for a couple of days' time and waved them goodbye.

My Sunday lunchtime appointment with chicken number one had gone well. I hoped chicken number two would be just as successful, although, somehow, I had lost my appetite!

Calving and Fitting

I had just finished a morning of fertility testing at one of our biggest dairy herds. As I gathered up my kit, I asked Jack, the farmer, about his calving time.

"We get very few problems calving cows here," Jack replied. "If we do have to call the vet, it's usually a tough one." We totted up the results of the morning's work: thirty-eight cows had been through the crush and most of them were pregnant. This did not surprise me, nor did it surprise the farmer – he had one of the best herds in the county and the management was second to none. It had been a good morning.

"Thanks Julian. I'll leave you to wash up your stuff. I need to go and feed the heifers and check the dry cows. I'll see you next week!" Jack sped away on his quad-bike with great urgency, as I set about cleaning my equipment and wellies. As I was loading everything back into my car boot, Jack came whizzing back with the same urgency as he had left, just ten minutes before.

"You're not in a rush to get off, are you?" he called. "It's this cow. She's on calving and something's not right." The question was somewhat rhetorical, since, even if I had been in a rush to get off, I would not have left the cow struggling.

I climbed into my car and followed Jack to the far corner of the field, where the cow was lying, trying to give birth. She was a quiet cow and I managed to examine her without having to fasten her up or corral her into a building. In the warm sunshine, it was a pleasure to peel off my waterproof top and my shirt to make the examination. Sure enough there was a problem. The cow's vagina spiraled around my hand like a corkscrew, which signified a uterine torsion. The uterus was twisted and the calf upside down. It was going to be hard work. However, after what seemed like too

long, I was beginning to make progress. Eventually and to everyone's relief, the new calf landed on the grass, narrowly avoiding a patch of nettles at the edge of the field.

"I told you that if we needed a vet it would be a tough one!" grinned Jack, and then added, "Thanks very much. That's been a good job." Praise indeed.

Later that day I turned my attention to the problems of much smaller patients. Itchy skin, grass seeds in ears and Labradors with sore hips. A busy afternoon surgery is cleaner and more controlled than much of our farm work, but no less challenging. My final patient of the afternoon was Bailey, a broken coated terrier.

"We've brought him in for his vaccine," his owners explained.

"But we wanted to talk about his fitting." They went on to tell me how Bailey had been suffering from sporadic seizures for the last few months, if not years. I made notes about the frequency and nature of these events and how long each one lasted. I needed to be as certain as I could be that the episodes were true epileptic fits. The point at which to subject a dog to a lifetime of drugs to control seizures is dependent on various factors, so I needed all the facts.

At the very moment that I started to press for precise details of the nature of each episode, Bailey started trembling.

"Oh, look!" exclaimed his owner. "He's just about to have one now!" Right on cue, Bailey demonstrated exactly what one of his fits looked like. For the second time in a day, the vet was right on hand!

An al fresco calving, and a very tough one. This cow had a uterine torsion, which I managed to untwist. Not easy but very satisfying.

Bonnie and the Magic Mushrooms

2nd August

There was much concern in Bonnie's household. Colin's daughter Laura, who was a member of the film crew for *The Yorkshire Vet*, relayed his worried messages and I arranged to see the patient the next morning. I'd seen Bonnie before to treat her stiff joints, so I knew her quite well.

The middle-aged Labrador, with her wide, appealing eyes, looked pretty normal as she sat with Colin and his wife Julie, gazing around the waiting room. I called them in.

She had been acting oddly since the previous evening, they reported. She was restless and unsettled, at times subdued then at other times uncomfortable. I asked all the usual questions, looking for some sort of clue. But her appetite was normal, drinking was normal, bowel habits and urination were ok. There was nothing to point me in any specific direction.

"She's just not right, Julian," explained Colin. Julie went on to add, "You know your own dog, don't you? So we are just a bit worried. She's not right."

I examined her all over. Her membranes were slightly pale and I thought I could feel some fluid in her abdomen, but there was nothing I could really hang my hat on. However, Julie was right – an owner does know their own dog and it is a foolish vet who ignores the gut instinct of an owner telling them that something is wrong. I admitted Bonnie for some blood tests and an ultrasound examination of her abdomen to look for the suspicious fluid.

By the end of the morning, I had my results: everything was clear. Bonnie's kidney parameters were just towards the top end of normal, but this was to be expected in a dog of her age. I called Colin with the good news. I suggested that they observe her behaviour over the next few weeks with a view to repeating the

Bonnie the Labrador – here in springtime, pre-mushroom season!

tests in a month's time. This would be a good way to check whether there was a more sinister problem emerging. Maybe though, it was just her arthritis flaring up?

After the phone call, I went back to see Bonnie. She was looking gloomy in her kennel. It was a sunny day, so I decided that, since she was the pet of a friend, Bonnie would make a good companion for a lunchtime walk along the river. Her behaviour during the walk was very odd. She pulled and tugged to get into the hedgerows and long grass in an erratic and almost manic fashion and I began to wish I'd left her at the surgery. After all, I don't usually take any of my patients for a riverside walk at lunchtime.

A couple of weeks later, I met up with Colin, Julie and Laura for coffee. They were passing through Boroughbridge and it was a good chance to catch up. Soon, conversation came around to Bonnie and her progress. "How's Bonnie getting on?" I asked. "It's nearly time to do another blood test, isn't it?"

"She's back to normal now," said Julie, but what she said next surprised me.

"Well, Julian. It's a funny thing, you know. We think we know what the problem was."

Colin went on to explain: "She's been a bit strange on her walks recently – frantically pulling me into the bushes. Then, just the other day, we caught her with something in her mouth. She'd picked something up from the bushes, and it looked like – well we are sure it was actually – a *magic mushroom!* Could it be that she'd eaten one and that was why she was so odd?"

Suddenly it all made sense. Poor Bonnie had been eating hallucinogenic mushrooms from the hedgerows! No wonder I couldn't work out what was the matter. There isn't a blood test for that!

Don't Lick Tin Lids

10th August

My first patient of the afternoon was a cat. She was waiting patiently in her basket in the waiting room. She had been booked in as an extra appointment, just before the start of afternoon surgery.

"How can I help?" I asked, as the basket was lifted onto the consulting room table.

"Well. There's blood everywhere," explained the gentleman who had brought her. "It seems to be coming from her mouth, but I'm not sure. The hall and living room carpet are a complete mess. I'm looking after her for my daughter, who's on holiday."

I have come to learn that, where cats and dogs are concerned, a little bit of blood goes a long way. Minor cuts or scrapes can seem very much more serious than they actually are. But even with this in mind, I was not expecting the sight that presented itself when I opened the lid of the basket. The base of the box was completely covered in blood – just like a tap had been left dripping all night. A lot of blood goes even further than a little. The situation was rather urgent.

I quickly found the problem. Or, at least, part of the problem. There was an inch-long laceration on the top of the tongue. I suspected the tuna-flavoured lid of a tin can was to blame. I've seen this sort of thing many times before – tuna cans in the recycling bin, with their razor-sharp edges, are an unexpected hazard to cats. I took our patient straight to theatre and, under anaesthetic, started to examine the injury in more detail. To my horror, there was a similar sized cut through the underside of the tongue. The tissue left connecting the top to the bottom was only about three millimetres wide. The bulk of the cat's tongue was hanging on by a thread.

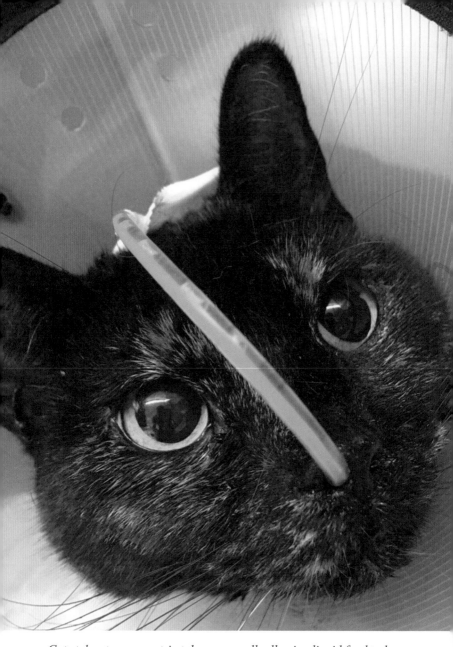

Cats tolerate nasogastric tubes very well, allowing liquid food to be given and avoiding the mouth. In this case, to allow the injured tongue to heal. This was the worst tongue injury I'd ever seen.

A debate ensued amongst all the nearby vets about whether this horrendous injury would be possible to repair. There was a very real possibility that both the nerves and the vessels supplying the end of the tongue had been irreparably damaged but, ever the optimist, I decided that I should try to fix it. I set about cleaning the area and working out how best to suture the damaged tissue back together. After a painstaking forty-five minutes, the cut edges had been re-apposed and the situation seemed immeasurably better.

The next job was to place a nasogastric tube. There was no way that the little tortoiseshell would be able to eat for at least a few days, even if the wounds started to heal as I hoped they would. Since she was still under anaesthetic, placement was relatively simple and the flexible, latex tube slid easily up one nostril and down into her stomach. I tested it by introducing a tiny amount of water, to make sure it hadn't entered the lungs. The tube was then anchored in place with special sutures, which I attached to the top of her head. Whilst these tubes look quite intrusive, most cats actually tolerate them very well. I administered plenty of analgesic and fitted a buster collar to stop her from scratching at the tube and pulling it out, and we were finally ready to wake her up.

I put her back comfortably in her kennel and made the phone call to relay both the bad and the cautiously good news. She was not out of the woods yet – very far from it. Yes, the tongue was back together, but would it stay together? Would the wound break down? Would proper function return? There was no merit in having a tongue if it flopped, out of control and unable to lap water. It was likely to be a long haul...

Summary Duties

17th August

The long summer evenings bring new challenges for a veterinary surgeon on call. Cattle and sheep are out at grass and, save for the occasional freak accident, are at their most healthy – free from the diseases associated with housing or the problems connected with having babies. Most of the emergencies at this time of year are dogs or cats. This was what made up the first part of my night on duty this week.

Moments after arriving home after evening surgery, I got my first call.

"I've just got in from work and my cat is not right. His hip seems painful," explained Casper's owner. Sometimes advice and reassurance are all that are required, but Casper sounded uncomfortable and needed to be seen.

As I headed back to the surgery, another call came in. This time it was a week-old pup with problems. I'd spent much of the previous weekend giving the aforementioned advice and reassurance about the impending birth of this very puppy. Everything had gone smoothly, without any need for veterinary intervention and seven chunky and very healthy bull terriers had arrived in the world. One of them needed my help this evening though, so I arranged to see it shortly after Casper.

Casper and his owner were waiting patiently outside the front door when I arrived. Casper was in his basket and his owner was in her work clothes – rather surprisingly, a blouse emblazoned with the snazzy logo of a nearby veterinary practice! I commented upon this with a grin as I set about checking her cat. It was hardly a glowing endorsement of her confidence in her employers! Casper, growling and hissing as I prodded his back end, had been bitten in a catfight. His temperature was rising and the ruffled fur and

*An English Bull Terrier pup, just a
few days old. Bullet-shaped but cute.*

punctures around his tail were sure to have been inflicted by a rival
Tom. Cat bites are contaminated with some nasty bacteria and can
quickly form into large abscesses. I administered some injections

and bade him farewell, with instructions to return the next day if he wasn't improving – or to take him into her own work, of course.

Then the pup appeared. Being just a week old, her eyes were still closed but she was strong and determined. I set about my questioning to find out the problem.

"Well, it's her mum," said the owner, concerned. "She's so good, she keeps licking and cleaning all the pups. But now, look! This one's navel is sore and I'm worried it will be infected. It's happened so quickly, but I think I've caught it early enough. What do you think?"

She was right. The little pup's navel was red, moist and already swollen. Her mum had unwittingly caused a major problem by her over-zealous cleaning. If infection gets a proper hold in a navel, it can track up internally, towards the liver. It was imperative to nip this problem in the bud. I reached for my antibiotics again and arranged another check-up.

I was soon back home and trying to make some tea, when I was interrupted by another small animal emergency. Although, it wasn't actually an emergency. It was speculation. Speculation about a cat's chance in a fight that had not yet happened.

"Charlie's got out. I had the door open to let in some fresh air and he burst out before I could stop him. He's not been out since the last time. You know, when he had his shoulder injured by the cat down the road!"

I remembered well. Charlie had been fortunate to escape with his shoulder intact.

"What I want to know is: what are his chances, Julian, if he gets into another fight? Could he win or will he need his leg amputating?"

I sensed that this caller was going to need a large dose of reassurance.

Two Pig Farmers Inseminating for the First Time

26th August

I had an email this week from the owners of a rare breed pig herd, for whom I had done some work a while ago. We had become good friends. They were hoping to supply sausages and meat to some swanky London shops and they needed me to provide confirmation of the high standard of welfare of their pigs. It was a great farm and the animal care was of the highest order, so it was easy for me to help.

After some to-ing and fro-ing, the final email appeared in my inbox, full of thanks – the black pudding would be taking its place on the breakfast menus of some of London's finest hotels. Before she signed off, Jess also related the story of a recent incident on the farm.

Jess and Mark needed to introduce some new genes into their herd. Rare breeds have a small gene pool, and this lack of genetic variation can lead to health problems. They had decided upon artificial insemination to improve the genetics of the herd and introduce some new blood, so to speak.

Jess's story went like this:

"Forgot to tell you about our first attempt at AI. I hope you're not eating!

"It was on our lovely, but obese, sow Clara. She's very dominant and now all the boars are scared of her, so I thought AI [artificial insemination] would be a good idea. I was at the head end, scratching her ears and Mark was at the business end, doing the AI. Well, she kept moving around and wouldn't stay still. I put my weight on her back, like you are supposed to, to get her to stand still, but every time Mark tried to insert the catheter, she kept fidgeting around. Eventually she settled, but after what seemed like ages, Mark said that the bottle of semen had not been taken in [usually the watery semen gets "sucked up" by the sow]. So, I said I'd get it in, and we swapped positions. Mark got on her back and scratched her ears and I took my place at the back end.

"I squeezed the bottle gently until all the solution was in the tube and then I pulled the bottle off and put my thumb over the end. Then, for some strange reason, I had the idea of putting my mouth over the end of the catheter, to blow the semen into the sow. I don't really know what possessed me!

"I was blowing quite hard and after a few seconds, I glanced up to see if it was all in and then I noticed the problem. I realised why Clara had been so unsettled when Mark was inserting the catheter. HE'D PUT IT UP HER BOTTOM!

"I stopped blowing and was about to give Mark what for. I couldn't believe he'd made such a stupid mistake! He'd been a farmer for forty years and surely by now he should know one hole from the other! Just as I started speaking, everything that I'd just blown down the tube came rushing back out and into my MOUTH! But worse than that, it wasn't just the contents of the bottle. I had, in effect, just given Clara a colonic irrigation – I will leave the rest to your imagination!"

By the end of this email I was rolling around with laughter. My last experience artificially inseminating pigs had been just as funny and I know that it can be fraught with minor problems, but this particular problem was a first! It was clear that Clara would not be getting pregnant on this occasion, so the forthcoming black pudding supply would be limited, but at least the pig was okay. I'm not sure about the farmers!

Calving and a Near Miss with a Wing Mirror

2nd September

The cow was prepped and ready for a caesarean when I arrived. My effervescent colleague Candela had attempted to deliver the calf but felt it was too big to be delivered naturally. She'd called for my help at half past eleven – not especially late, although I was already asleep, because one half of the family had set the alarms for 5am to get to a rowing regatta. It was the Northern Sprint Championships and Jack, my eldest son, fancied his chances. I had already offered my advice: "Be brave". Rowing sprints need not just strength, power and technique, but also steely determination to hang on as the lactic acid starts to burn. Since I was on duty again, I couldn't go along to watch and would have to rely on text updates during the course of the day's racing.

So, I abandoned my early night and headed out to help Candela.

"It's all ready to go," she reported. "But please, would you like to feel first. I think it's big, the head is back and I can't get it out. But you might be able to?"

I was happy to have a feel, although I didn't want to undermine her initial assessment. The calf was big, as she had said, and its head was back – a challenging calving if ever there was one. But, experience told me it was worth a try. A natural birth is always preferable for the cow, quicker for the tired vet and cheaper for the cash-strapped farmer.

Eventually, drawing on all the techniques I have acquired over the years, I managed to get the calf's head up and into the mother's pelvis. First part sorted. Now we just needed to get it out.

The cow, by now, was very cross. She was not appreciating our help. We decided to put her in the cattle crush. This is not always the best thing to do for a calving, but under the circumstances, it was the safest option. In the darkness of the night, everything

*Persuading the patient and its newborn calf back into
the correct place was not easy. I was in the safety of my
car at this point and my wing mirror was still intact!*

seemed more difficult and it took some persuasion, but eventually
and reluctantly she went in. Working together, with Candela
operating the calving jack and me keeping the head in position,
we managed to deliver the huge calf. We congratulated ourselves
as we made it comfortable in the calving pen. Everything had gone
well and it looked as if we would soon be heading home. After
tidying up our equipment, we opened the crush to let the cow (who
was still very cross) out to join her baby. It ought to have been
fairly simple – she would walk out through the opened gate and
turn left into the calving pen where her calf was waiting and all
would be good. Unfortunately, she had other plans, which did not
involve finding her calf. She burst out of the crush, turned right
instead of left, and charged past Candela's car, past my car –
missing my vulnerable wing mirror by a whisker – and away into
the pitch-black yard, with its gate open to the road. Suddenly,
everything was not so simple. The calf was out of the cow, but the
cow would very soon be out of the farmyard. Everyone started
running, shouting and panicking. More by luck than judgement,
she swerved into a blind ending corner of the yard, penned in by
tractors and a combine harvester. Fearing for my wing mirrors
again, should she make a dash back in my direction, I decided that
my time on the farm was now done and made my excuses. As I
reversed out, the two farmers managed to corral the annoyed cow
safely into the pen and my wing mirrors were out of danger. The
other good news? Exactly twelve hours later, Jack became the
North of England under-17 single sculls sprint champion.

It's Not What We Thought

8th September

"SEE ASAP – dislocated toe," it said on the computer, next to Barney's appointment. Barney's worried owner was on her way to the practice with the bouncy pointer. He'd suddenly gone lame. Very lame. He wouldn't put his back foot to the ground at all.

I asked the nurses to set up the X-ray machine in anticipation of some sort of orthopaedic injury. A broken or dislocated toe, similar to the familiar football player's injury, would be extremely painful. An X-ray would identify exactly the nature of the problem.

When he arrived, it was clear which leg was affected. Barney was as lively as ever, but he was only standing on three legs.

"He was fine this morning," reported his owner. "He went out in the garden and was playing with his ball. Then he yelped and came back into the kitchen hobbling. I think he's dislocated his toe!"

It sounded a plausible explanation, and I knelt down to examine the toe more closely, before we sent him for the expected X-rays. His foot was massively swollen, looking more like a balloon than the end of a limb. The skin around the toes was distended, glistening and red, deepening to purple in places.

"I don't think this toe is dislocated," I ventured, to the obvious surprise of Barney's owner, and to the disappointment of the nurses, who had been anticipating an exciting repair.

"Is there any chance he could have stood on a bee?"

"I suppose so. There are bees in the garden," she nodded, somewhat deflated after having rushed her dog to the vets' amidst such drama.

I administered a strong steroid injection and applied some cream, with instructions to come back again the next day for a follow-up. I was confident his foot soon would be back to normal size.

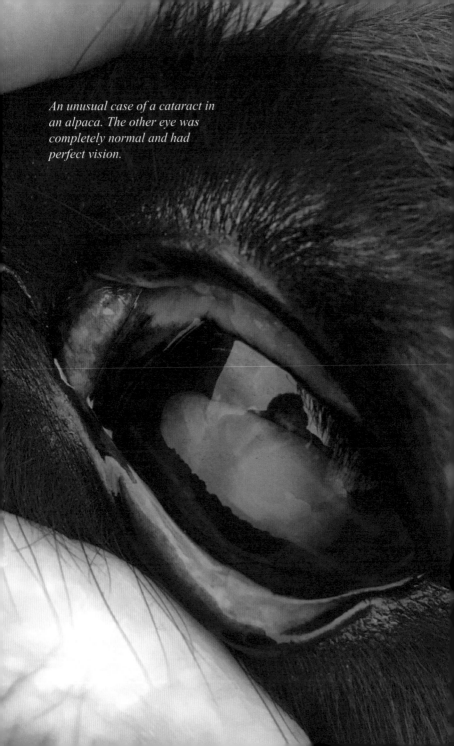

An unusual case of a cataract in an alpaca. The other eye was completely normal and had perfect vision.

Later in the week, I had another case of "it's not what we thought". I was visiting a herd of alpacas, to administer a plasma transfusion to a two-day-old cria. A Cria is a baby alpaca. If the mother does not have sufficient milk, or if the baby is weak or doesn't suckle properly, the newborn cria can become deficient in the protective antibodies that usually come from its mother's colostrum – the first milk. This leaves it vulnerable to life-threatening infections. Experienced alpaca breeders prepare for this eventuality by arranging with the vet to collect blood from adult alpacas in advance. The plasma is then separated off and frozen. This is exactly what Jackie and I had done a few months ago, in anticipation of the arrival of lots of babies, and this week I was back, to give the life-saving (or at least a life-enhancing) plasma.

It went very smoothly. The catheter placement was perfect and the cria sat on Jackie's lap, comfortable and relaxed, as the plasma ran in. Once we had finished, the little baby went trotting happily off to see his mum. He already looked energised.

The next alpaca to look at was an adult with a bad eye.

"It's all cloudy," explained Jackie.

I gathered what I thought I would need and went to see the alpaca in the field. It was sure to be a corneal ulcer, I thought, just like those I'd seen recently in a number of llamas, caused by the irritation of dust from fields, thrown up as combine harvesters did their work. Corneal ulcers cause an obvious cloudiness and are painful.

As I approached the animal, it certainly didn't look in any pain. I peered into the eye and, even without the benefit of a darkened room and an ophthalmoscope, I realised that, for a second time this week, it wasn't what I had expected it to be. There was no corneal ulcer. The cloudiness was in the lens. This camelid had a cataract.

Alpaca, Head Out

16th September

We had planned a practice meeting for Wednesday evening. There were a few things to discuss, not least the new rota, and it had proved impossible to find a time during the day when everyone was free for an hour. At least in the evening we should all be able to concentrate, without the distraction of sick animals and the telephone.

So, it was bound to happen – the best laid plans and all that! At ten past six, just as evening surgery was drawing to a close, Julie came off the phone and into my consulting room.

"It's an alpaca that's having difficulty giving birth. Can you go straight away?"

The meeting would have to wait. I love delivering any baby animal, but delivering a newborn alpaca – a cria – is particularly satisfying. They are usually born easily without assistance, so it's not something I get to do very often. However, when things do go wrong, they go very wrong, so delivering a cria (amusingly known as "unpacking") is full of challenges. Emma, my colleague, and another Emma, our current vet student, were as excited as I was and asked if they could come along. We went in convoy, through Bishop Monkton towards Harrogate. The farmer was standing in the field and waved me in when he spotted me. Even from a distance I could see my patient, a lovely white female. It looked as if she had two heads, because the partially born cria was stuck, with its head and very long neck dangling out. As I approached, I could see the baby's head moving around and its eyes blinking. It must have been very confused, in its half-born state. The reason for the difficulty was also clear – there was only one leg lying next to the head and neck.

This was a bad thing to see, because it meant that the other leg was bent backwards, rendering the cria completely stuck at its shoulders. It could only be born if I could straighten out the bent leg. This is straightforward in a lamb, where it is quite a common cause of dystocia, but everything about an alpaca is long. Its neck is long and so are its legs. The pastern – the bit below the fetlock – is particularly long, and this was the bit I would need to straighten out.

I got a bucket of water and added some antiseptic, and applied plenty of lubricant gel before I made my first tentative examination. After some gentle manipulations and with baited breath, I managed to flip the offending leg up so it was pointing outwards, in the correct position. The next bit should have been easy, but the baby was still quite difficult to deliver because it was so big. To everyone's relief, the cria, quickly identified as a girl and christened "Olivia", finally slithered out onto the grass. Her enormous eyes could look around more freely now and it wasn't long before she was tottering to her feet. With an ungainly head perched on a long, wobbly neck and with a confused expression, Olivia looked just like ET, in the 1980s film, as he tried to "phone home".

All was well and the two Emmas couldn't quite believe what they had seen. An alpaca giving birth is a unique experience! I cleaned up my kit and myself and we made our way back to the practice to drop off student Emma, before finally heading to the practice meeting.

My colleagues did not look too concerned about the delay – the rapidly emptying bottles of wine and bowls of crisps and nibbles told me all I needed to know.

"Sorry I'm late," I apologised. "I've been busy unpacking."

"Unpacking" a cria is always difficult. Legs and neck are very long and it's hard to unravel the baby.

Torsion of the caecum is a rare and serious problem for a cow, necessitating immediate surgery if there is to be any hope. My patient walks back to the field and we all cross our fingers.

Start of a Run: Caecal Torsion

21st September

Thursday was the mid-point of a run of five nights on call. That doesn't sound so bad. Plenty of people work five nights in a row. As a veterinary surgeon though, it's not just the nights that we cover, but also the days in between. And it's not as if the days are quiet either. What you don't really need, at the end of evening surgery, is a cow with a twisted intestine.

She had been off it all afternoon (I knew the feeling) but Tim, the farmer, couldn't put his finger on the problem.

"She doesn't want to come in to be milked and she looks poorly," he explained down the phone. "She's quite bloated, too." It wasn't much to go on. Adult milking cows do not usually suffer from the classic and easily fixed bloat that affects their younger counterparts, usually as a result of overeating the wrong sort of food. So, as I headed out to see this mystery cow, despite my fatigue, I felt a surge of anticipation.

Sure enough, the cow, still lying by herself in the field, looked awful. Her nose was resting on the ground – a sign that she felt too weak to lift her head. As I started to examine her, she struggled to her feet and began slowly to make her way towards the farm buildings. It was a walk she knew well, as this herd used a robotic milking machine. The cows were free to walk from the fields to the parlour whenever they wanted to be milked.

My initial examination didn't tell me much, other than an elevated heart rate, but once we had ushered her into the crush, it was the rectal examination that yielded more information. I could feel a large, distended part of the large intestine on the right – this was not normal. It was tight and painful, and prodding it caused my patient to let out a low-pitched "moo".

I listened with my stethoscope over the corresponding area on her right flank. High on this side I could hear a high-pitched pinging, characteristic of a section of the intestine full of trapped fluid and gas. I made a diagnosis of a caecal torsion – the cow equivalent of a severe case of appendicitis. We briefly discussed the options. The prognosis was grave. She had zero chance of survival without surgery, but to operate was also risky and carried no guarantee of success. But Tim wanted to do everything we could.

"Well, we have to give her a chance, don't we?" he said. "She's the one you saw back in February with the really bad foot. She recovered from that and she's a good cow. You'd better crack on."

Tim's facilities were fantastic. The shiny new cattle crush even had an opening door to allow me access to her right side, and I had soon clipped, prepped and anaesthetised the area ready for surgery. Sure enough, just as I had expected, the affected part of bowel was full of gas, distended and fluidy. I made an incision into the over-stretched caecum, releasing the most enormous amount of gas and stinking brown liquid, trapped there because of the twist. Then I repaired the incision and, with eyes closed to help me visualise the direction of the twist, I unwound the torsion. The rest of the operation was routine, closing the muscles and skin. This bit, at least, I'd done hundreds of times before. As for the diagnosis and untwisting of the caecum – this was just my second case.

Tim and I, and the assembled onlookers who had variously appeared during the operation, all convinced ourselves that she looked better as she picked her way back to the field than she had on her way in. Only time would tell.

The Birds and the Bees

28th September

It has been very busy over recent weeks. Dogs and cats seem to be multiplying – sometimes literally – and farm work, which is often quiet during the late summer, defies the usual seasonal trend and continues to fill our days.

One of the jobs that has demanded my attention this week is the fertility testing of tups. It is not too long before the breeding season starts for sheep, particularly for breeds like Suffolks, which can start lambing as early as Christmas. With tupping time upon us, it is important to check whether the male sheep, who often have a large number of ewes to cover in a six-week period, are "firing on all cylinders".

In contrast to cattle, where a farm often only has a single bull, tups are usually put with the ewes in small groups, so one individual ram who is infertile, or sub-fertile, can go sometimes undetected. However, it is possible to test individuals by collecting a semen sample and analysing it down the microscope. It is a relatively simple procedure and the tups seem unperturbed by the process. I have tested seven tups on two farms in the last two days and the biggest trauma they suffered was when they jumped over the gate, or charged at each other as they returned to the grassy fields.

On day one of testing, I saw three rams. Two of the samples were fantastic – future breeding career guaranteed – but one (whose donor had the telltale soft testicles) failed. That ram will be retiring soon. On day two, I tested four tups. All the samples were brilliant – motile and beautiful. I love being able to move my makeshift lab sheep-side. To be able to look at the basic building blocks of life – gametes, carrying the chromosomes of a future living creature – is an amazing thing. Life-sized sheep producing the cell-sized germs of a new lamb, both just as visible with the help of the correct equipment. It always gives me a thrill. It is science in action.

Back at the practice, during afternoon surgery, there was more new life (although this time not quite so new) in the shape of a litter of eight-week old puppies, in for their first vaccinations. The pups were fluffy and cute and keen to burst out of their wire basket. There are a number of crossbreeds that are popular at the moment, which have cute names that add to their appeal. I think these pups were cavacockapoos, although I may have misheard. I'm guessing some combination of Cavalier King Charles spaniel, cocker spaniel and poodle. Whilst all these new crosses masquerade as proper breeds by virtue of their cool names, they are actually still crossbreeds. However, in my opinion, this is a good thing, because crossbreeds are generally uber-healthy and more likely to be free of some of the nasty hereditary diseases or congenital problems that we sometimes see in highly bred pedigrees. Their parents do not need to be DNA tested to ensure freedom from disease, nor do they require hip or elbow X-rays, because the mix of genetics is fantastic and should eliminate some of the problems associated with a small gene pool.

As I took my time over the last couple of pups in the litter, I asked about the breeding process.

"It was very simple," replied the owner. "I just took my bitch to the dog when I thought she was ready. They got down to it in the back garden. It was quite nice really – it was a lovely sunny day. I had a cup of tea, then we came home. Now, seventeen weeks later, here we are."

In this case, there was clearly no need for a fertility test. Nature had done its thing and done its thing well.

Definitely the cutest patient of the week!

Russell the Albino Hedgehog

5th October

"Have you ever castrated a hedgehog?"

It was an unusual question.

Lucy, an excellent student from the Royal Veterinary College, had been with us for a couple of weeks, learning the ropes of mixed practice and picking up valuable tips for her future career. I like teaching vet students, especially those who are keen and enthusiastic. Lucy had enthusiasm in abundance. Her question took me by surprise. I have castrated many animals, of all different types and sizes, but never a hedgehog.

It is an important job for a vet. Just watch any episode of *The Yorkshire Vet* and you'll see for yourself! Castration prevents unwanted behavioural traits and tendencies, avoids accidental pregnancy and, in some cases, reduces the risks of diseases that are connected with having testicles.

I wish I had started a log book at the beginning of my veterinary career, recording all the procedures I had carried out – castrations, spays, calvings, caesarians, night-time calls and so on (in fact, this is one piece of advice I give to budding veterinary surgeons when they see practice with me). If I had done this, I am certain that castrations would feature most frequently. I'm sure I would be into the tens of thousands of testicles by now. A busy morning's ops list might include five or six dogs or cats to castrate – that's ten or twelve testicles – but a big batch of young calves could tick off as many as fifty or sixty in a day. Add in a smattering of ferrets, guinea pigs, rabbits and the odd colt to geld and my tally must surely be into five figures. Ten thousand divided by 22 years makes just less than 500 castrates per year. That makes just ten per week, which doesn't sound very many. I think I do more than that. Like I said, I should have kept a logbook.

Anyway, a hedgehog was not on my list and I asked Lucy why she wanted to know.

"I have a pet Albino hedgehog," she explained. "He's lovely, but he gets very aggressive with people he hasn't met before. I was wondering if you thought it might be helpful to get him castrated. Would it calm his aggressive tendencies?"

The theory was a good one, and I thought it would certainly help if the aggression was territorial. Castrating rabbits does wonders for their temper issues and is often recommended by vets. A hedgehog shouldn't be too dissimilar, should it?

I had to confess, though, that I could not comment with authority. On the subject of pet hedgehogs, Lucy had more experience than I did. I was, however, intrigued by the little pet. From the photos on Lucy's phone, he looked very friendly and exceedingly cute.

"Maybe you could bring him in?" I suggested. "I'd love to see him and I can check out his testicles." This was not a sentence I thought I'd ever hear myself saying to a vet student, especially not about a hedgehog.

So, the next day, Russell the albino hedgehog made himself comfortable in the kennels. The TV crew from *The Yorkshire Vet* assembled, sensing a story to be filmed. Another castration but on a new species. Tick.

I introduced myself to Russell, expecting a hostile response from the ASBO hedgehog. We made friends and Russell let me examine him. I was confident that the surgery could be undertaken simply and safely, but as we played and as I took my obligatory selfie (#albinohedgehogsofinstagram), Russell was so friendly that I just couldn't bring myself to put the little spiky pet under the knife. The hedgehog had a reprieve!

I think both Lucy and Russell were quite relieved.

Another selfie with an unusual patient. This time Russell the albino hedgehog!

Peter the tup had an appointment to be castrated. He also had a magnificent set of horns.

Castrating Peter

11th October

Peter had been a prolific tup in his time. He had fathered a whole generation of Hebridean ewes at the farm in Nun Monkton, where he lived. As a result of his efforts, the small flock of this unusual breed had expanded rapidly. The farmer and his wife were very fond of the tough tup, but now they were faced with a problem – all the ewes they needed to get in lamb were Peter's daughters. They needed a new ram. But what to do with Peter? There were three options for the old boy:

1) Peter lived by himself, alone in a field, enjoying his retirement but with no friends.

2) Peter was sent to the butchers to make some rather tough, mutton-based meals.

3) Peter was castrated by me so he could retire gracefully and stay with the flock, without the risk of any inbred lambs appearing.

Doug, the farmer, had been mulling over these options and asked for my advice. Castrating an adult ram is not a procedure that is done very often. Male sheep have disproportionately large testicles and removing them is fraught with potential problems. However, an appointment with the butcher did not seem like a very palatable option, and nor did a sad and lonely retirement without any friends. The latter actually sounded like the very worst option.

I found myself agreeing to a rather challenging operation. My Plan A was to have Peter in at the surgery, so that I could carry out the procedure under general anaesthetic, using gas. In this way, I would have better control over the situation. Although I hadn't met Peter, I knew that, though his testicles were sure to be large and plump, being a Hebridean sheep, he would actually be quite small in stature. Gassing to sleep a large sheep, such as a Suffolk or Texel would be a ridiculous idea, but a small one, only as big as a Labrador, would be feasible.

However, when he arrived in the back of the trailer, Plan A turned out to be a stupid idea. Peter had large horns and, when I went to say hello, he put his horned head down and charged at me with malicious intent. So much for trying to be friendly! A cross tup in the operating theatre would end in disaster. I quickly formulated a Plan B which involved no anaesthetic gas and no perilous visit to the inside of the practice. I decided that I would use the trailer as a makeshift operating theatre. Instead of a general anaesthetic, I would inject local anaesthetic into the area and use a device called a "Burdizzo" to do the op. A Burdizzo is a piece of equipment best described as a vice-like clamp. It is applied to the cord of each testicle, crushing the cord and obliterating the blood supply to that testicle. It was invented in Italy at the beginning of the last century (presumably by Mr Burdizzo?) and the design and process hasn't changed since.

I sat Peter on his bottom in the trailer and Doug held his feet. After cleaning the area and instilling some local anaesthetic to numb the skin and the cord, everything was ready. Usually I would clamp in two places on each cord, but Peter's testicles were surprisingly large, so for extra safety I put three crushes on each side. I patted the tup on his horny head after I'd finished and gave him an extra dose of painkiller. I didn't want him to be sore over the next few days. By way of thanks, Peter charged at me again. Luckily, his horns made contact with the side of the trailer rather than my leg.

All in all, castrating Peter hadn't been so bad after all.

Jay with the Bladder Stone

18th October

Jay was my first patient during evening surgery. The note on the appointment list said he had cystitis, a provisional diagnosis made by the receptionist booking the appointment, so I had something of a "heads up" before he even made it onto the examination table.

"He cocks his leg, but then he stands there for ages," explained his owner, worried and confused in equal measure. "Sometimes a lot of wee comes out. Sometimes just small squirts. It doesn't seem painful, but it makes our morning walk take ages. I was late for work yesterday because he took so long."

Urinating more frequently and struggling to pass a full and continuous stream are classic signs of bladder disease. Jay's owner had, sensibly, brought a sample in a plastic tub and when I tested it, the dipstick showed there was an abnormal amount of blood in the dog's urine. Simple cystitis, whilst seen quite frequently in a female, is relatively rare in a male dog, so a thorough examination was required to identify a reason for the blood. Starting at the head, I worked back. When I got to his abdomen, the problem became clear. Jay's bladder was painful and there was a firm, conker-sized object sitting in the middle of it. I immediately suspected a bladder stone, so arranged for him to come in the following day for X-rays. If I was right, he would need surgery to remove the offending stone or stones.

The X-rays were conclusive. The stone was clear to see, sitting right in the middle of Jay's bladder.

Bladder stones are fairly common in dogs and arise for a number of reasons. A combination of urine composition and pH, urinary stasis, bladder infection or incorrect diet can lead to a build-up of minerals. This can then result in the formation of tiny, gritty stones, which sometimes grow to a considerable size. The process is

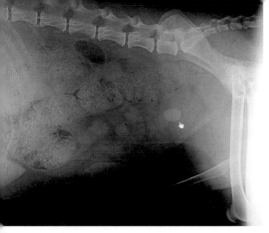

Jay had a large, calcified stone in his bladder, causing all sorts of problems. The stone develops from minerals which form crystals and then grit-like deposits, leading onto stones.

similar to what happens when a kettle fills up with limescale. Solid bits precipitate out of the urine and that's when problems develop. In male dogs this can be particularly serious because the small stones can get stuck behind the bone in their penis. Bladder obstruction can ensue with its obvious and serious consequences.

Regardless of what had caused Jay's stone to develop, it needed to be removed. The surgical procedure, called a cystotomy, is straightforward but removing a solid thing from the inside of an animal never fails to provide excitement for everyone in the building. The stone was soon out and sitting in a kidney dish rather than sitting in Jay's bladder, to a general buzz of amazement.

He recovered well and went home later that evening, with some very relieved owners. But the story of a stone doesn't end there. Once it has been removed, it is important to find exactly what it is. The stone is sent to the lab to be laser-sliced and analysed to see what the core and the shell are made out of. With this information, we can instigate a corrective diet to modify the composition of the urine – its acidity and the mineral content. This can help to dissolve mini stones and individual crystals that might still be left, too small to be seen in the bladder or on an X-ray, and this stops further stones from developing. There is a lab in Minnesota, in the US, who test bladder stones free of charge. So, as I write, the stone from the bladder of a dog in Whixley, is winging its way, airfreight, to America.

The Westie without a Waist

26th October

"Thank you for seeing him, Julian. I am not sure what is wrong. He's just getting bigger. He's lost his *waist*. He might be just fat, but I wanted to get him checked," explained Duffy's owner.

I had seen this problem before – a cute West Highland white terrier, getting on in years, a bit more sedentary than he had been, but adept at persuading his doting owners to donate extra morsels in his direction. However, once he was on my consulting room table, it became evident that the cause of his problem was not so benign. I could feel a mass, a large tumour in the front part of his abdomen. I tried to relay the serious news as gently as I could. This was anything but a Westie with a fat tummy. We agreed that I should take some X-rays that afternoon so we could formulate a plan. I explain to all the vet students that come my way that there are seven "F"s of abdominal distension (and one other, which doesn't begin with "F"). Only the best students can crack this list. It seemed likely that the reason for Duffy's abdominal distension was the one that didn't begin with an "F".

The X-rays and scan confirmed the presence of a melon-sized mass, although it was not clear what it was attached to. Surgery would be required, but not until I had reinforcements. My wife, Anne, with whom I work every Thursday morning, would need to help me with this exploratory operation.

Breakfast was rather tense the following morning, because I knew that Anne and I would be up against it to sort out little Duffy.

In came the patient, waddling along beside his owner, who squeezed my arm as she handed him over.

"I know you'll do your best, Julian, but if it's too bad, if there's no hope, then do what is right for my little man." Her parting words were tearful, but sincere.

I nodded my agreement and understood exactly what was inferred.

I took Duffy to theatre and set up his drip. Once he was anaesthetised and on the table, the full extent of his abdominal distension was even more marked. While it looked dramatic, the outcome depended more upon what the mass was attached to than its size. In general terms, if a mass is associated with the spleen, the outcome can be favourable – although not necessarily. If the mass is on the liver, the outcome is usually terrible, as it is often inoperable. Whilst surgeons like to know exactly what they are dealing with, using scans, X-rays and blood tests to help make a definitive diagnosis, it is only when we reach for the scalpel that we can really see exactly what is going on. So much as we like to work everything out beforehand, surgery is very often the answer.

And it was today. As soon as we could see inside the abdomen, it became evident that the poor little Westie had an enormous tumour invading his liver. Despair was soon followed by a glimmer of hope – it was attached to just one lobe. Would it be possible to remove the lobe and the mass together?

We thought we could.

Two painstaking hours later, Duffy was waking up from his anaesthetic, while part of his liver and the huge tumour were sitting in a kidney dish. His tummy was a fraction of its former self and I picked up the phone to relay the cautiously happy news to his owner. It was the start of what was sure to be a long recovery, but so far so good.

Gardening Gloves in the Bowels

31st October

Afternoon surgery was already overflowing when an extra patient appeared, to add to the list. Wilfred the Labrador peered out, sadly, from under a chair in the waiting room, looking both guilty and poorly at the same time. The notes on the computer told only half of the story:

"Labrador vomited two gardening gloves."

I called the owner and his son into the room and began my interrogation.

"And you're *definitely* sure he vomited two gloves out? And they were both completely intact?" I quizzed, to firm nods from both owners.

"We know there were two that came out, 'cos we checked them. Definitely two," confirmed the son. "That was the day before yesterday," added his father. "But all of today and last night he's looked out of sorts and can't keep any food down."

Wilfred's gloomy face and tense abdomen suggested there was something else stuck. I set about palpating his tummy. Despite the tight abdominal muscles resisting my probing, I could feel there was something very wrong.

"We'll need to do some X-rays to see if there's anything else in there," I said. "Leave him with us and we'll get on with it this afternoon."

The X-rays showed a funny stripey thing, causing an obstruction in Wilfred's abdomen. Surgery would be required for sure. What on earth was down there? More garden accoutrements? I could not think of any other gardening equipment that would be as tasty as gloves. Not that gardening gloves would be at the top of many people's list of favourite snacks.

Before long the very hungry Labrador was ready for his operation. I made a long incision to facilitate a thorough check of all the parts of his stomach and bowel. A dog's intestine is very long and, when looking for a foreign body, it is crucial to follow it all the way from stomach to rectum. I was expecting to find the offending article in the stomach, but the red-verging-on-purple colour of the first part of his small intestines highlighted the region to investigate. At its centre was a distended area, which warranted attention. As I cut through the bowel wall, an alien-like object appeared. Slowly but surely a lime green, very smelly, very rubbery thing emerged, finger by finger, as if it was waving. It was a bright green gardening glove. A third one to add to the collection. We always clean up and keep these foreign bodies, sealed up in a clear plastic bag, to give back to the owner. This gardening glove smelt so bad that, even after cleaning, two plastic bags were required. I am not really sure why we thought we should give it back – I was certain it would never be used again.

As I repaired the intestines and closed the muscle layer and the skin – a painstaking job because the incision was so long – conversation in theatre turned to speculation about why a dog would eat a gardening glove. A colleague related a story of a dog who had eaten a pair of tights. It had vomited one foot whilst, at the same time, passing the other foot out of its bottom, the gusset (not a word I've ever used before) still being stuck in its stomach. Whole crab apples don't do a dog's insides much good and neither do rubber doorstops – all things we have had to remove after a hungry dog has swallowed them down without a second thought.

And there still remained the mystery of the fourth glove – had it been chewed up into finger-sized portions, eaten and passed? I had visions of a frustrated gardener cursing his poor memory, or maybe even his wife, for misplacing his favourite pair. Or, at least, half of his favourite pair.

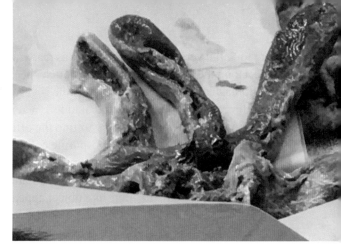

Slowly but surely a lime green rubbery thing emerged, finger by finger, as if it was waving....

One of the silkie hens suffering from rhinitis, sinusitis and conjunctivitis. It's not always easy to treat this condition successfully.

Silkies in the Sauna

4th November

I had finally got to the end of a big batch of TB testing on a family farm, helped by most of the family. As it was half-term, there was a selection of kids on hand, all farming fanatics and all keen to get involved. It was Ben's tenth birthday, so I'd given the young farming enthusiast the job of writing down numbers for me in my notebook. It was a useful job to do and a perfect one for a young assistant.

As I washed my wellies, I chatted to Ben about his interest in farming. He told me all about his fledging hen enterprise – how he was building up his small flock, how he sold his eggs to passers-by and how he had a selection of special hens called silkies. I asked him about the health of the birds and how he looked after them. The knowledgeable young lad knew lots about his birds and was very aware of the problems they might face.

"There are a couple that have gone blind though," he said. "Dad says there's not much to be done. They don't seem too ill, but they aren't getting any better." He looked puzzled.

"There might be things that we can do," I suggested. "Are they on the farm? I can have a look at them if you'd like?"

They weren't on this farm, which was his grandmother's, but Ben (well, Ben's mum) offered to bring the affected birds into the practice so I could have a look at them. I was optimistic (as usual) that I could help. I thought it was possible they might have a condition called sinusitis which had glued up the eyes with gunk, pus and mucous. If this was the case, then treating the infection, opening the gummy eyes and relieving the pus might solve the problem.

Two days later Ben, his mum and his three hens arrived for their appointment. I called them into the consulting room, anxious to examine the birds to see what I could do.

As I expected, the birds had pretty severe sinusitis and five out of six sets of eyelids were stuck together. Some gentle bathing with moist cotton wool and cotton buds allowed me to coax open the gummed-up eyes and things looked much more promising. I gave each bird an injection and prescribed powder to mix in the water. Ben's egg sales would need to be put on hold, until the eyes were better, the medication finished and the appropriate withdrawal period observed.

The next thing I prescribed was not a medicine. But it was a treatment of sorts – one that I thought would help, but not one I'd ever suggested to the owner of some chickens before. I advised Ben to take the three chickens and put them in a very steamy bathroom. I suspected I would need Ben's mum to be in agreement for this to happen. I could just imagine my mum's reaction if, when I was ten, I had said,

"Mum, I'm just bringing in three hens and I'm going to put them in the bathroom and turn on the shower so that the steam can decongest their sinuses." An animal-lover as she is, I am not convinced this would have met with approval. Luckily for Ben and his chickens, Ben's mum was game, and keen to help sort out the snotty silkies. Ben promised to give me an update on the progress of the birds.

As I waved Ben, his mum and his birds goodbye, I sensed that not everyone was as confident as I was that there would be a favourable outcome. I felt sure, however, that the three blind hens would be back running around the farm in no time at all.

Three Little Birds

9th November

On Wednesday of this week, we saw three little birds. This was not a re-creation of the famous Bob Marley song, but the reality of a day as a mixed practitioner in a typical independent and traditional practice in North Yorkshire.

The first two were already in the diary. A rescue centre for birds of prey in the North East had contacted the practice. Two birds, under their care, had died suddenly. They needed to have post-mortem examinations on both birds and had been struggling to find a veterinary practice that would or could help.

"The trouble is, they've all gone corporate," explained the exasperated staff member, who had been charged with driving south to deliver the dead birds. "Nobody is interested in doing a post-mortem examination. Thank you so much – you're the first practice we could find who has been able to help us out."

I felt like apologising for the disappointing apathy that had clearly descended on some members of the veterinary profession to the north of Boroughbridge, but it wasn't a problem for which I could claim any responsibility. I cannot condone the changes that the profession has undergone in recent years, and all I could do was offer my best help under the circumstances.

Both of the birds had been very old – the vulture in its late twenties and the buzzard approaching forty, but since they had both died without warning and at the same time, the rescue centre needed to confirm that nothing was amiss. Although I wasn't an expert on birds, I would at least be able to try to ascertain the cause of death and obtain samples to send to the lab if I was in any doubt. Both had been in the freezer for a week or so, but had been given the chance to defrost before my appointment. I met the birds and their custodian, Steph, outside the practice, as I returned from my lunch break.

Steph handed over the large polystyrene box in which the birds had travelled and, several minutes later, I had one diagnosis – the buzzard had a precariously thin heart wall, a large amount of fluid within the abdomen and a swollen liver. These were classic signs of right-sided congestive heart failure and this was almost certainly the cause of death. The vulture, however, left me guessing. There were no obvious lesions. I hoped old age was enough of a reason to put on the certificate.

Carrying out post-mortem examinations made rather a depressing start to the afternoon, but it quickly improved with the appearance of the third bird – a barn owl, brought in by a lorry driver. The owl had collided with the lorry, leaving it injured and stunned by the side of the road. In a collision between a lorry and an owl, there is only going to be one winner. The beautiful bird was limp and lifeless, swaddled carefully in a towel and nestled in a box by the lorry driver, who wanted to help as best he could.

"It's been floppy and limp ever since I picked it up. I think it's badly injured. I feel awful – it just flew out and I crashed into it. I hope you can sort him out?" the poor man said, clearly upset by the accident.

I carefully picked up the swaddled bird, worried that this might be the third bird of prey not to make it out of the practice today. As I started my cautious examination, the bird opened its eyes, stretched its wings, took off and did a full circular lap around the consulting room, before landing gracefully on the table. This was an immeasurably happier ending to the day's encounters with birds than I had expected – and for the third bird, for which I didn't need to administer any treatment! He'd recovered by himself.

Accidents in the House

16th November

Monday was a day filled with interesting cases. Several of these involved the toilet habits of dogs. Bladder disease and problems with urination are common in cats, and often difficult to deal with, but today was all about dogs. Dogs wetting the bed, pooing in the night and, finally, not pooing at all.

First was Jess the Labrador. Her stiff hind limb gait, the grey hair around her muzzle and the bluish hue to her eyes, all suggested she was elderly, even before I checked her records. She was in for an annual check-over and vaccination and my initial questions quickly found a focus on her weak bladder.

"Well, she can't really hold on through the night at the moment and her bed is often wet in the morning," confessed Jess's owner, with some concern. It was an inconvenience both to Jess and to the humans in the house, but I sensed it was a problem viewed as one of old age, rather than a medical issue. I probed a little further with my questions: was it always during the night? Did she leave wet patches during the day where she had been lying down? Was Jess drinking more than usual? Did she need to wee more frequently and did she have any difficulty when she did?

I was trying to establish whether the wet bed was due to urinary incontinence, where urine leaks without any control, or because Jess's bladder was full for more of the time because her thirst had increased. Alternatively, it could have been the result of a bout of cystitis, which leads to an urgency to pass urine so that the dog just cannot hang on. Often, the answers to these questions give us much of the information we need, before we even start our clinical examination.

The next stage was to palpate Jess's abdomen, and her bladder. Several years ago, I was called upon to examine a basset bitch to see if she was pregnant. This usually involves an ultrasound scan, but I always like to feel with my fingers first. Old-fashioned, I know, but fingers attuned to palpation rarely let a physician down. On this particular occasion, before I had chance to feel any puppies, my fingers fell onto a bladder so full of stones it felt like a bag of marbles! I surgically removed the offending pebble-like stones and for years they lived in a plastic bag in the fridge of my consulting room, from where I would retrieve them with a flourish, whenever I needed to explain to someone the dangers of bladder disease.

Anyhow, Jess had a normal, smooth, non-painful bladder, so I was happy stones were not part of her problem. Handing over a kidney dish and a plastic pot, I instructed Jess's owners to take the elderly dog for a short walk outside to allow the collection of a urine sample.

Five minutes later, they were back, carefully balancing the metal dish, half full of slightly sploshing urine. A dipstick told me the answer – Jess had cystitis. This would be easy to fix with a course of antibiotics.

I scrolled down my appointment list and was surprised to see another dog, Toffee the Jack Russell, with a similar toilet problem. However, Toffee's overnight issues were of the poo variety.

Our computer system has a small space next to the name of each patient, for a description of the reason for their visit. Next to Toffee's name was a brief but odd summary of his problem, which was one I wasn't sure I 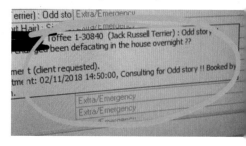 would be able to fix: *"Odd story. Since the clocks have changed, dog has been defaecating in the house overnight??"*

Maybe the dog's clock needed to go back to BST? It might offer a simple, though unconventional, cure!

This was the strangest lampshade on a dog I had ever seen!

Lampshades on Dogs

22nd November

I've never been a fan of putting a lampshade on a dog. Or a cat, for that matter. A lampshade (technically called a Buster, or an Elizabethan Collar) is frequently required to stop a pet from licking its wound, as this hampers the healing process but, as a rule, animals absolutely hate them. And even if they do attenuate to the large satellite-dish arrangement round their neck, the back of the owner's calves and the door frames of the house certainly do not.

Styles and designs have evolved over the years. The classic is, of course, the clear, stiff plastic version that attaches to the collar. The see-through nature is supposed to make it easier for the patient to see through it, maybe, just maybe, convincing the dog that he isn't wearing it at all. More bad news for the door frames.

The soft, floppy version is an attempt to save the calves and the furniture, but mainly it just makes the dog look like a flower. The last one I used had a pug in its centre so it didn't even look like a happy flower. There are blow-up ones, like the rubber rings that might be used to help a toddler in the swimming pool. The theory is that the ring limits movement of the neck, stopping the dog from bending round to reach its wound. They don't work very well, but at least offer some protection in case of aquatic accident. There is a variation on this that looks like one of those neck braces people used to wear after car accidents in the 1980s. The poor dog's head is held rigidly forwards, making it actually (and literally) a pain in the neck, because the dog can't steer.

One former colleague, for reasons unknown, used to recommend using an actual bucket, with its bottom cut off. A gloomy Labrador looks even more tragic with a bucket strapped to its head with baler twine.

But the latest designs for protection of wounds employ a completely novel concept. After an op, some of our patients now leave the practice wearing a body suit, something between a baby-grow and a triathlon suit. The head is free to move but the pesky tongue can't get to the wound. Dogs seem to like wearing them, especially in winter. We haven't put a cat in one yet. I'm not sure how that would work.

However, comfortable and practical as canine all-in-ones are, they don't work if we have to stop a dog rubbing his eye, or scratching his ear with his back foot. Buster collars are still the only thing for this.

I saw a boxer this week, following surgery to remove a mass from his eyelid. Typical of a boxer dog, he barged in, clouting the door frame and his owner with the edges of his Buster collar. Then he started to have a sneezing fit. Well, you can imagine the chaos – legs, snot and a hard plastic collar smashing all over the place. But then he came up with a solution. He pushed his collar firmly onto the floor, making a sturdy base to sneeze into. It also helpfully contained the spray.

My final visit of the week was a sad one. Elsie the bulldog had passed away during the night. She had been a regular visitor since I started at Boroughbridge and both the dog and her owners had become very good friends. As we spoke about the sad demise of one of my favourite patients and reminisced about the funny things she had done, I admired a quite magnificent lamp in the conservatory. Its base was a bulldog, made of china, and the lampshade was on its head, covering the bulb, which emerged from between its ears. Despite the sad occasion, it was very funny and we laughed about its appearance.

"Julian, if it reminds you of my lovely dog, you can have it!" declared Mrs Taylor!

So now it's sitting in the kitchen, reminding me of happy times. I have seen many lampshades on dogs, but never one like this!

Fun with an Autocue

It is Monday morning and I'm writing this on the train to London King's Cross, after a busy weekend on call. In the last seventy-two hours, I have stitched up a nasty wound on a spaniel, treated fourteen heifers suffering from an outbreak of pneumonia, put down an elderly Jack Russell, rescued a cat from the jaws of renal failure and seen a goat with mastitis and a giant rabbit with an abscess, amongst other things.

I have been on duty – either on first or second call – for the last ninety-six hours. This is not a terrible thing; when you are a vet in mixed practice, it's something you get used to.

But the moderate level of anxiety that is connected with the unpredictability of being on call – not knowing what the next phone call will bring or whether, when you go to bed, you will sleep for six hours or no hours – is nothing compared with the anxiety that is with me now as I head to London to film some "VT" for a Channel 5 telethon. It is the channel's first ever telethon and it will be raising money for five animal charities. The live show, of which I will be part, will feature proper television stars like Jo Brand, Ben Fogle and Gaby Roslin. It's called *Help the Animals at Christmas*.

When I get to London, I am going to film some clips to show the work of the Blue Cross. I think my job is to talk to the veterinary surgeons from the charity to find out about their work, which today will be from a mobile clinic, offering access to veterinary care for owners who might otherwise find it difficult. I also have to do a "down the lens" piece, which is what professional TV people do. You know how it goes: "Hello, I'm Julian Norton from Channel 5's *The Yorkshire Vet*..." This is very different from the way we film *The Yorkshire Vet*, where we definitely don't look into the camera. Since it's an observational documentary, looking into the

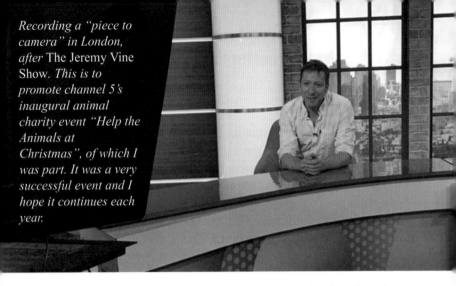

Recording a "piece to camera" in London, after The Jeremy Vine Show. *This is to promote channel 5's inaugural animal charity event "Help the Animals at Christmas", of which I was part. It was a very successful event and I hope it continues each year.*

lens or referring to being "on telly" crosses what is referred to as the "fourth wall" and it isn't to be encouraged. Luckily, I know the director for today, so I hope she'll help me out.

Then, on Tuesday, once we've done the VT for *Help the Animals at Christmas*, there is more discomfiture. It will be an early start, because I'm going to be a guest on *The Jeremy Vine Show*. This is two hours of live television. There are lots of cameras, a studio audience, an autocue for the proper presenters and five newspaper articles for me to review along with some discussion of topical issues and current affairs. At least, that was the format before, when it was *The Wright Stuff* with Jeremy's predecessor, Matthew Wright. It's a far cry from a weekend on duty with a batch of coughing heifers and the chance of a nocturnal emergency. Which is harder? It's difficult to say. The first time I was on *The Wright Stuff*, I was utterly terrified – my comfort zone wasn't just on a different page, it was in a different book altogether!

But today, worry about the cameras or not, at least my beeper isn't going to go off to send me to calve a cow. However, I do have my stethoscope, just in case while I am commentating on the mobile veterinary clinic, my actual veterinary skills are called in to action! I think I'm better with a stethoscope than with a microphone!

An Old Friend

7th December

Opposite the veterinary practice in Boroughbridge, there is a baker's shop. Next door to the baker's there is a butcher's. It is a shame there is no shop that makes candles! There is, however, one of almost every other type of shop in this lovely town. The baker's is a popular spot, although not one that I frequent often because, sadly, I can't eat gluten. The upstairs window, though, is sometimes used to film shots of me, or my colleagues as we leave the practice to go off on our calls ("Julian is heading out on an emergency call," I hear Christopher Timothy explaining to viewers of *The Yorkshire Vet*.)

The owner of the baker's came in this week with her cat, a noisy Siamese called Ronnie.

When I was in the sixth form of school, I had a girlfriend who had two Siamese cats. Katie (the girlfriend) was lovely, but our relationship was hindered by the Siamese cats, who hated me with a vengeance. They growled and meowed and hissed, persistently and aggressively, which caused terrible tension every time I visited. So, whenever I see or treat a Siamese cat, I am reminded of their involvement in that happy-but-ultimately-doomed-to-fail teenage romance.

I put these thoughts behind me and called Ronnie and his owner into the consulting room. I was surprised by the appearance of an old friend. I hadn't seen Bert for about ten years – he had retired and I had moved on – but it turned out that he was Ronnie's owner's father. I knew him well from my previous life as a young vet in Thirsk. Bert was the farm manager at a fantastic sheep and beef farm that nestled at the bottom of the tree-lined slopes that joined the flat Vale of York to the Hambleton Hills. I used to love my visits to this farm, because Bert was such a kind and wise old farmer. He looked to me for veterinary expertise, but in truth I

Ross, the cameraman, ever alert to a new angle, films the practice from the upstairs window of Havenhands the bakers, opposite.

learnt more from him than he did from me, and this was something for which I was extremely grateful. He always wore a trilby hat and, true to form, he was still wearing one today. I was delighted to see him and we immediately started to recollect past visits and shared anecdotes, reminiscing over previous successes and failures.

"You remember that calf, the one that was lying flat out in the field. I said it was abart buggered, but you said you thought you could fix it – AND you did! I never thought that calf would come right, but it bloomin' well did!"

"And what about that heifer that was calving, up at the shed near the woods?" I added. "That was a long night, wasn't it?"

Eventually, I turned my attention to the cat, putting our stories to one side. Ronnie had been in a fight, as was his tendency. There were two big wounds, scratches verging on lacerations as a result of the skirmish.

I admitted him to the kennels. He would need an anaesthetic and surgery, albeit fairly simple surgery, to clean up and repair his injuries.

"And you needn't worry," Bert reassured his daughter, as I took the cat one way and she and her father headed the other way, out of the door and over the road. "I know Julian will do a good job. Just like he did on that Kerry cow, up on top o' t'hill that morning."

It was touching that Bert had remembered our treatment of the sick cow that morning. As for the Kerry cow, that's another story all together…

A Cat and a Velodrome

14th December

Last weekend was a weekend free(ish) of veterinary stuff. We were heading to London. December is a popular time for trips to London, to go Christmas shopping or to see a show. For family Norton, however, it was neither the theatre nor the shops that brought us to King's Cross. It was the weekend of British Rowing Indoor Championships, held in the Olympic Velodrome.

The mere mention of the phrase "British Rowing Indoor Championships" brings me out in a cold sweat. Exactly ten years ago, I took part in the very same event and it was, without a doubt, the hardest six minutes and fifty-two seconds of my life. As I collapsed next to my machine at the end of the race, I vowed never to return. Yet here I was. However, this time I was only slightly nervous. My two sons bore the brunt of the nerves, for both Jack and Archie were racing, and I was watching. I had every confidence they would surpass my moderate achievements of a decade before, and I was glad to be sitting in the stands.

Around one hundred Concept2 rowing machines were lined up in the centre of the velodrome, all connected together. Big screens relayed the times of each competitor and the spectators could watch the virtual boats race along those screens. We all cheered madly, although in the turbo-charged atmosphere there was zero chance of being heard. Amidst all this, I kept anxiously checking my phone for messages, because the previous day I'd had a call from a friend whose cat I used to treat.

"Longtail" was the apt name for a cat who was, apparently, twenty-six years old, making him the oldest cat I have ever treated. The geriatric cat and his owner, Rebecca, had moved from North Yorkshire to London recently and his health had taken something of a nose-dive after the move. I'd offered advice over the phone, based on the blood results that Rebecca had relayed to me but, as the cat was at the other end of the country, there was little I could do for him in practical terms.

"Are you working this weekend?" Rebecca persevered. "If so, I'm going to come up to Boroughbridge to see you. Those injections you used to give him always worked wonders. The vet in London doesn't have any and won't order it in. I think it would help and I'd love to give it one more try. I'd do anything to help him."

I explained that I wasn't working at the weekend, but suddenly realised that I would, in fact, be somewhere near to Rebecca's house. Or at least, nearer than I would have been, in Boroughbridge. Everywhere in London is connected by underground trains – surely it would be easy to meet up?

"Well," I said, "by bizarre chance, I'll be in London on Saturday, so if you can bring him over to the Olympic Velodrome, I can see him if you'd like? I won't have all my kit for a full examination, but I can easily bring an injection with me."

A plan was hatched. It sounded very good in principle, but in reality I wasn't sure it would be a good idea to a) bring a twenty-six-year-old cat on the tube or b) for me to inject it whilst inside, or indeed outside, the Olympic Velodrome. It made an interesting topic of conversation over dinner, when we met up with friends in a restaurant in Westfield on the Friday night, before the championships.

So, Saturday morning came and as my lads got ready to row, Rebecca, Longtail and I also had our concerns. I'd never treated a cat in a velodrome before. I hoped it would go smoothly!

Jamie and the Bloated Bull

22nd December

I had an interesting companion this week. As well as the ever-present camera team following me around, I had a work-experience student to keep me company. Jamie's parents are family friends, who live in the French Alps. Jamie was keen to spend a week watching the workings of a vet in North Yorkshire. I collected him from Thirsk station on a damp and grey Monday lunchtime. It was a far cry from his Alpine home, where he would have been surrounded by snowy mountains and deep blue skies

He would be staying with us at home all week and by day would be watching and learning at the practice. I hoped we would be able to keep him busy and that he'd be suitably entertained. He'd travelled a long way to get here! It didn't take long before he was into the action. Our first patient of the afternoon was a dog who had swallowed a small rubber ball. It had become lodged in the intestines and the more the bowel contracted to try and move it along, the more wedged it became. An exploratory laparotomy was needed to remove it. Jamie was adept and enthusiastic with the camera on his phone, taking a series of action shots of the surgery. He also scribbled away, taking notes in his notebook. He explained that he had to do a presentation about his work experience to his school, upon his return. In both French and English!

A day of travelling alone in a foreign country, meeting everyone at the practice, watching operations for the first time and making his copious notes meant Jamie headed straight to bed after a rather late tea, completely exhausted. I didn't ask him if he'd like to be woken up during the night to come with me to lamb a sheep. He was keen but not that keen.

Consulting for most of the next day was not quite so exciting, but a trip out with a colleague to see a ram with a broken horn was a particular highlight – lots of blood! Later on, the excitement

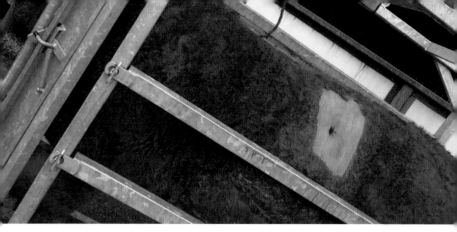

ramped up again, with a very urgent visit to see a cow with bloat. Jamie had to move over for Ross's and his camera, but watched in earnest, even before we got cow-side, as I answered Ross's questions about the seriousness of the situation. It was no exaggeration to explain that yes, this was extremely serious and, if left untreated, the animal would certainly die.

We arrived at the farm in a hurry and everyone bundled out, much to the surprise of the farmer. He was not expecting to see a vet followed by a cameraman, a soundman and a French boy. We quickly made our way to the bull, already expanding to fill the cattle crush, its sides bulging through the gaps between the bars. I discussed my plan with the farmer – there are different ways to treat bloat – and then explained this to Ross (aka the audience of *The Yorkshire Vet*) and then to Jamie, who was furiously scribbling notes, taking photos and avoiding the TV camera all at the same time. My plan was to create a ruminal fistula. This is a hole, made into the rumen, its edges sutured to the skin, to provide a semi-permanent outlet for the build up of gas that was becoming trapped.

It is a quick procedure, a lot of hissing and a very foul smell later, the bull had regained his normal, streamlined figure. The crisis was over and he looked much happier.

"Do you know French for 'ruminal fistula'?" asked my able young colleague. At that point, I was finally stumped.

Taking a Patient to the Pub

30th December

It was Friday night, and another night on call. The microwave had just "pinged" to tell me that my shepherd's pie was ready. At that very moment, my phone made the same noise as the microwave and I knew that the meal would need to be re-heated later, for a third time. I had a Labrador to examine. She had a wound on her abdomen, which sounded as if it would need to be repaired surgically.

Aggie jumped out of the car at the surgery, followed by her owner with his son, who was eager to make sure Aggie was going to be okay. The wound was nasty. The edges were gaping and already starting to curl and dry up.

"I'll need to have her in for an hour, maybe more," I explained. "Can you come back at about ten-ish? I'd normally suggest you go to the pub, but I guess maybe not tonight?" I wasn't sure the son, who looked about twelve, would be interested in an hour in the pub. However, Aggie's owner grinned:

"I'm glad you suggested that," he replied, "because that was exactly our plan. Come on son, let's go for a pint."

So, Aggie's nearest and dearest went for some Christmas father/son bonding in the pub next door, while I took the Labrador to theatre.

Once she was asleep on the table, I clipped the hair away from the edges of the wound, thoroughly cleaned it with surgical scrub and prepared for surgery. I didn't have a nurse to help me, but there was something calming about working on my own in the quiet building, with only the noise of the ticking clock, rather than the usual hustle and bustle of daytime in a veterinary surgery.

The wound looked much better once it had been repaired – I even took a photo in case anyone on Instagram was interested. Then I

The Black Bull in Boroughbridge – the perfect place for a festive pint, whilst waiting for your dog to recover from its operation!

administered the reversing agent, so Aggie would wake up promptly. Modern sedation is brilliant. We have powerful drugs that work both if given intravenously or if injected into the muscle, which is often very convenient, especially in a wriggly animal or if you are on your own as I was tonight. Even better, we can reverse the sedative effects with an antidote, enabling dogs to go home shortly after what can be relatively major intervention.

So, by the time I had written up her notes, Aggie was sitting up and looking around. I found the paper on which I'd written her owner's mobile number, and was just about to call them when I then realised that I knew where they were. I locked the front door, switched off the lights, put Aggie on her lead and left via the back door of the practice. For the first time ever, I took a patient to the pub.

It was just a twenty-metre walk.

"Can you bring dogs into this pub?" I asked a couple of customers, who were enjoying a cigarette and the festive Christmas lights of Boroughbridge, outside The Black Bull.

"Of course yer can," was the answer I needed.

The Black Bull was the first place I ever visited in Boroughbridge, about twenty-five years ago – although that's a completely different story. I made my way through its bustling rooms searching for the father and son combo, who I knew would be surprised to see me with their dog in the bar.

"Ah, Aggie! Is she OK?" came a call from a table in the corner. There was much tail wagging and general relief. "Thank you so much for bringing her! Can I get you a drink?"

I would have loved to have stayed – under different circumstances, without being on duty, it could have been a long and festive night and a perfect way to bring to a close my first year in Boroughbridge!

Epilogue

The fifty-two short stories in this little book started life in my weekly column in *The Yorkshire Post*. Each one describes an interesting case or two from the week. Sometimes, while I am buying a sandwich in Boroughbridge, or when I am on a farm, someone will ask, "What did happen to that cow?" or, "Was that cat alright in the end?" So, I thought it would be an interesting conclusion to *On Call with a Yorkshire Vet* to provide a short epilogue, with "What happened next…" for some of those stories that were left hanging.

Barry's cows DID have iodine deficiency. They were treated with both iodine boluses and some iodine pour-on. A pour-on is a simple method to boost iodine levels in cows, as the iodine is absorbed through the skin. Barry was happy to do this to his Simmental cows, which already had brown backs, but wasn't so keen to pour it onto his bright white Charolais, which would look a terrible mess after the sticky brown liquid had been applied.

The lacklustre chameleon was "110% better", according to his owner, after his injection, dietary modification and new hydration system, although I still couldn't get him to change his colour like on the cartoons!

In other reptile/chelonian news, Toby the tortoise made a full recovery, after a few days of stomach tubing, bathing and an array of tasty treats. He finally munched on a coriander leaf of his own accord. I visited later in the summer, to find him marching around a sunny lawn, filling his wrinkled face with dandelion leaves. He had been a very satisfying case.

Mia the meerkat made a full recovery, despite her much shorter tail. Surveying the savannahs of Great Ouseburn was not so easy, but she found a new bunch of friends and enjoyed a happy life. I've seen her again for a follow-up check – she's looking for a new mate, so maybe I'll see her again before too long.

The horse with colic – in the middle of a day chock-a-block with horses – confounded my pessimistic diagnosis of grass sickness. At my follow-up visit later that day, I found her munching away at her hay net and the gut sounds had recovered to full health.

In veterinary medicine, the successes are always tempered by sad outcomes. My evening cow with a twisted caecum, for all she was much better after the relief of gas, did not make it through the night. Both farmer and I suspected this might happen – she was very sick and the surgery was a long shot, but one we were both willing to take. Also, for the cat under the hedge, her injuries were so great there was no hope of recovery. I did find her owner – she was only metres from her front door – and they asked for the contact details of the man from the pub, so they could thank him for finding her. At least her last hours were warm and comfortable rather than alone in a ditch.

On a more cheerful note, Peter the Hebridean ram did, finally, enjoy a happy retirement, surrounded by his friends. At least, he did once his testicles had shrivelled up and disappeared. His dotage would be a contented one.

Duffy and Sid – the enormous liver tumour and the kidney cancer patients respectively – both rallied spectacularly. I saw them both regularly over the following months and became great pals with them both. Courtesy of Duffy's owner, I enjoyed the finest bottle of Burgundy I've ever had!

My little tortoiseshell with the lacerated tongue, despite naysaying from some colleagues about her chances, lapped at food within a week and recovered to full health. She was an amazing case and testimony to the incredible healing powers of both cats and tongues. She has not been near a tin lid since.

Gary's penis looks amazing, now the tumour has fallen off – my rubber ring technique worked a treat.

Erin the vet student, who helped me calve the cow with the bizarre water bag, is loving it at vet school and making fantastic progress; so too is Hannah with her Sunday lunchtime chicken. I've seen her since with her dog. I think the future of veterinary practice is in safe hands.

My cria unpacking went well. Olivia, as she became known, developed slightly odd front legs, but her appealing eyes and tottering gait brought her national adoration, featuring as she did on *The Yorkshire Vet* during series seven.

Help the Animals at Christmas made a whopping seven-hundred thousand pounds in just three hours, for worthy animal causes. Impressive for its first airing. Let's hope there's many more to come.

The seven 'Fs' of abdominal distension? Food, flatus (wind or gas), fluid, foreign body, foetus(es), fat, faeces. And cancer is the odd one out, because it doesn't begin with 'F'.

Oh, and the Wagyu steak from Topcliffe was delicious!

Acknowledgements

Once again, I have David Burrill and his colleagues at Great Northern Books to thank for publishing this, my fourth, book and for his skilful cover design and layout. My oldest son, Jack, for the cover photo. It makes a pleasant change to see a vet book without the main protagonist clutching his beloved pet. This time Emmy, my faithful Jack Russell, looks on with excitement.

Again, thank you to my new friends, clients and colleagues in Boroughbridge. Without you all and your animals, this book wouldn't exist. Thanks to Ben Barnett and everyone at *The Yorkshire Post*, for continuing to have interest in my weekly column about my veterinary life, upon which this book is based.

Thanks to Paul Stead and his enthusiastic team at Daisybeck Studios and also to Channel 5 for their continued support of *The Yorkshire Vet*. Were it not for this popular observational documentary and my involvement in it, I imagine not one of my books would have appeared. 2018 has been challenging for me in many ways and I'm grateful to Paul Stead, in particular, for his unswerving confidence in my ability to hold the series together.

Once again, thank you Anne. Writing this last bit now, we are both sitting at the kitchen table, tapping on laptops for the final editing of *On Call with a Yorkshire Vet* with the fire roaring and a gale howling outside. We'd have never guessed this is how we would be spending a Sunday morning!

River Swale

Skipton

Dallowgill

Galphay

M

Pateley Bridge

Markington

Greenhow Hill

River Nidd

Harrogate

Almscliffe
Crag

River Wharfe

Colli